Dedicated to the two most inspiring and supportive
people in my life... Mum and Dad

ISBN-13: 978-1540678324

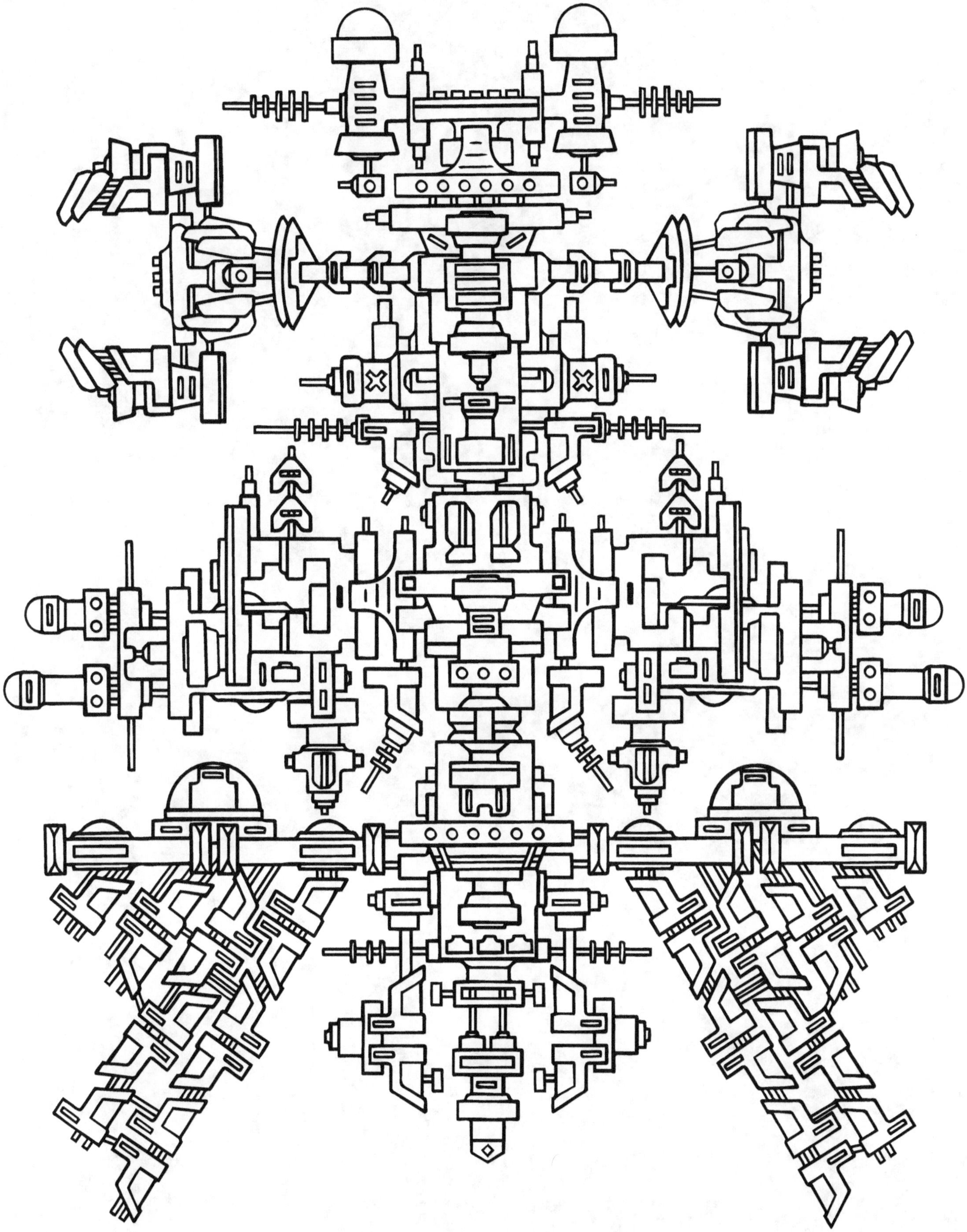

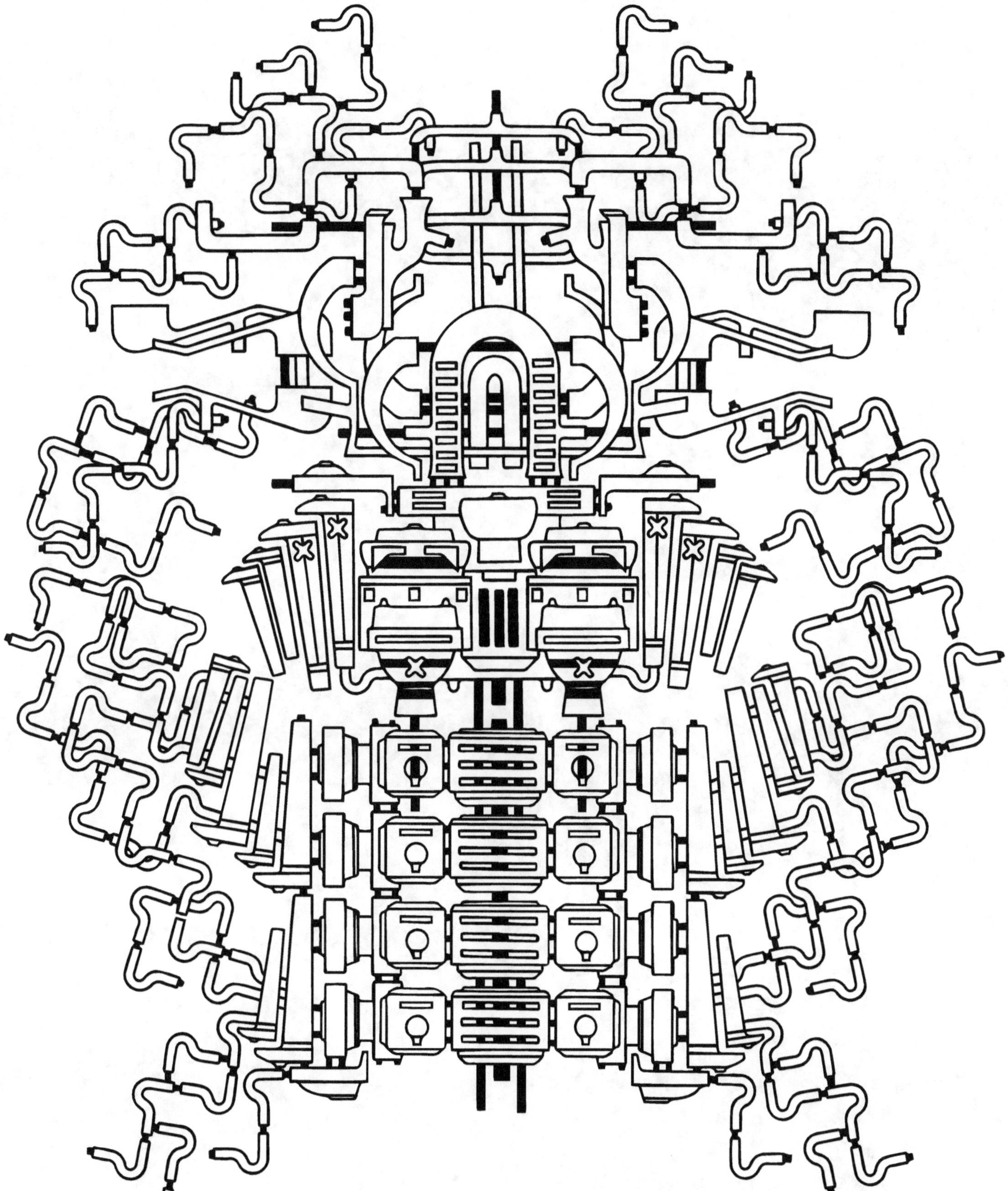

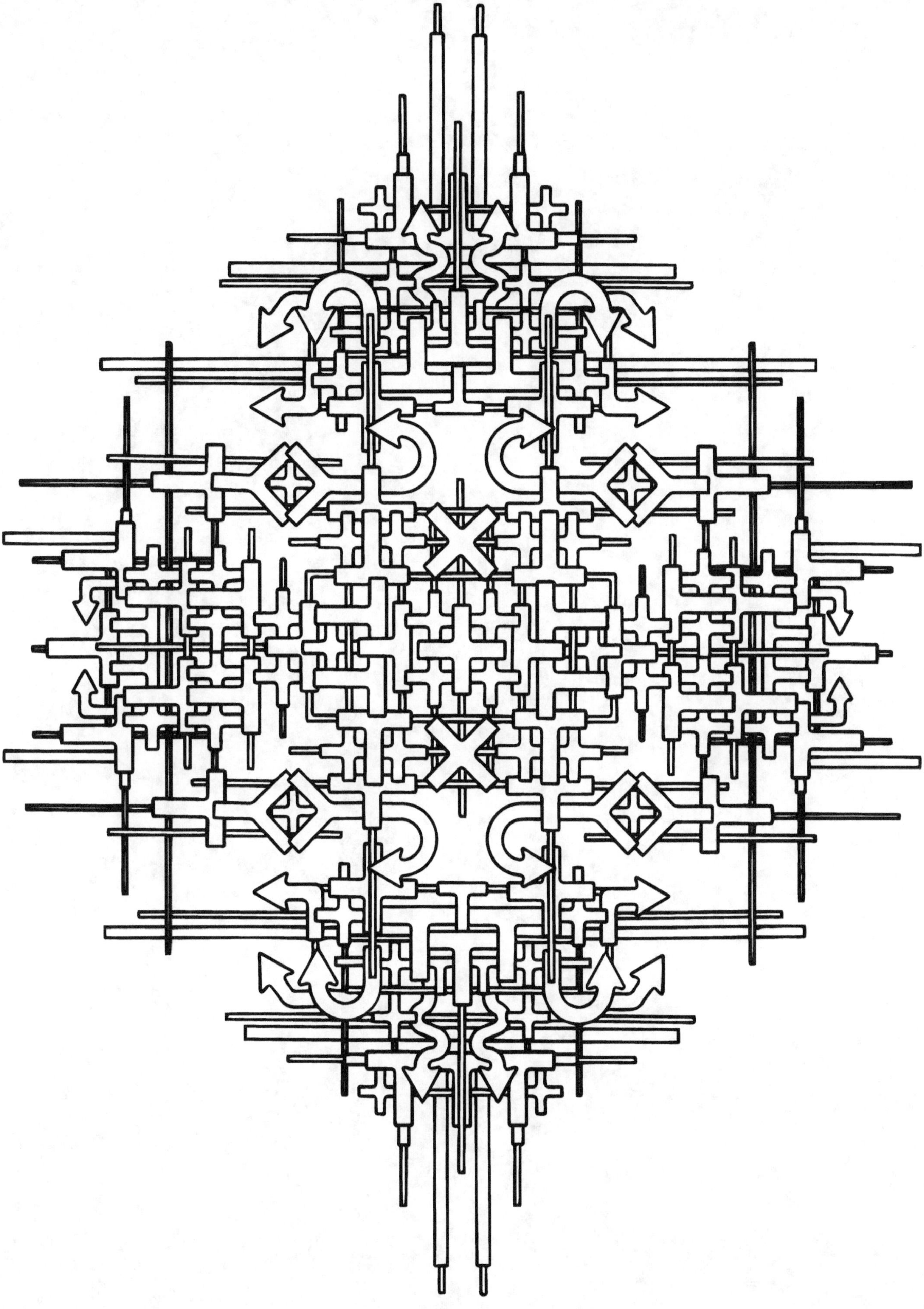

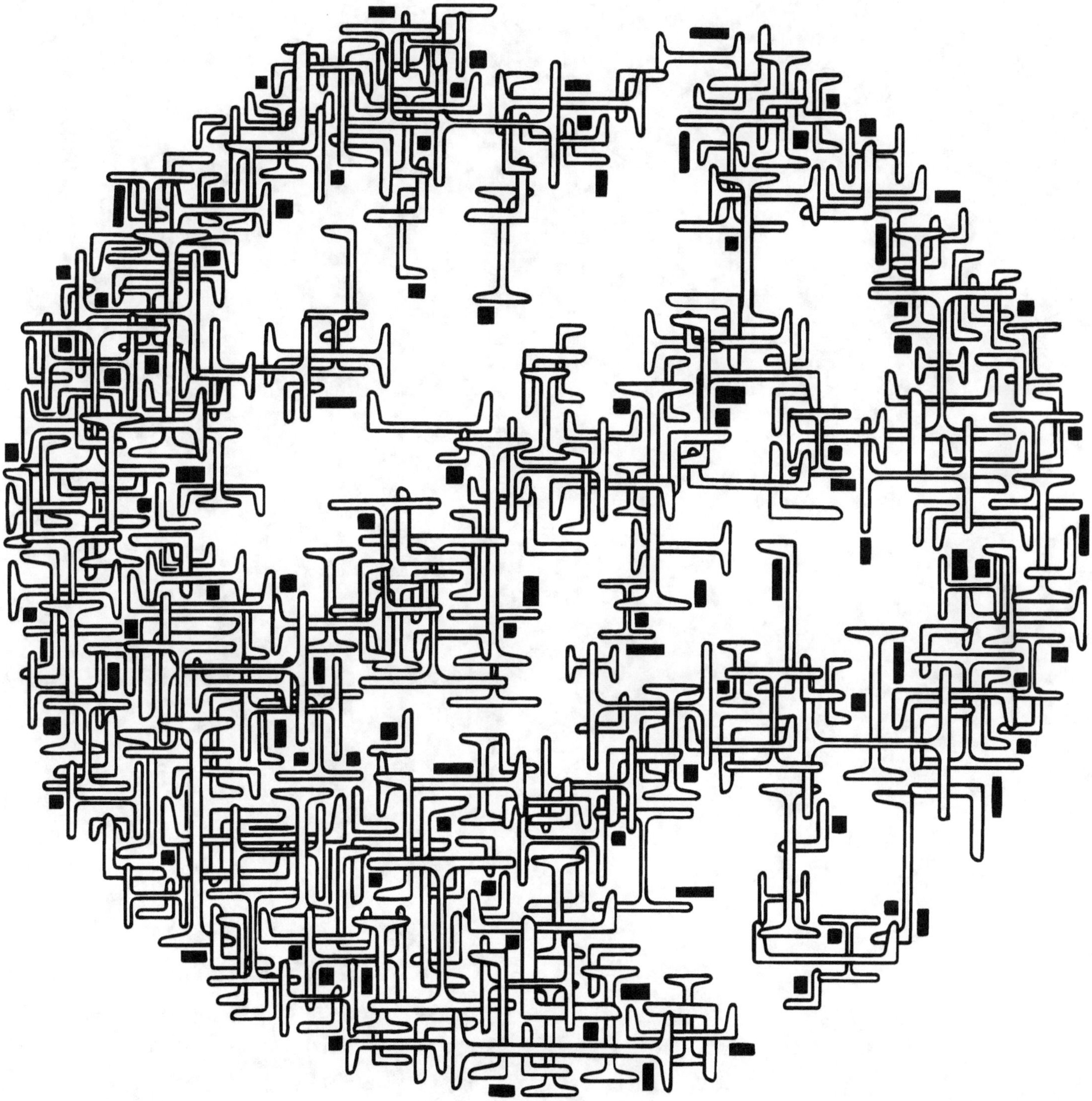

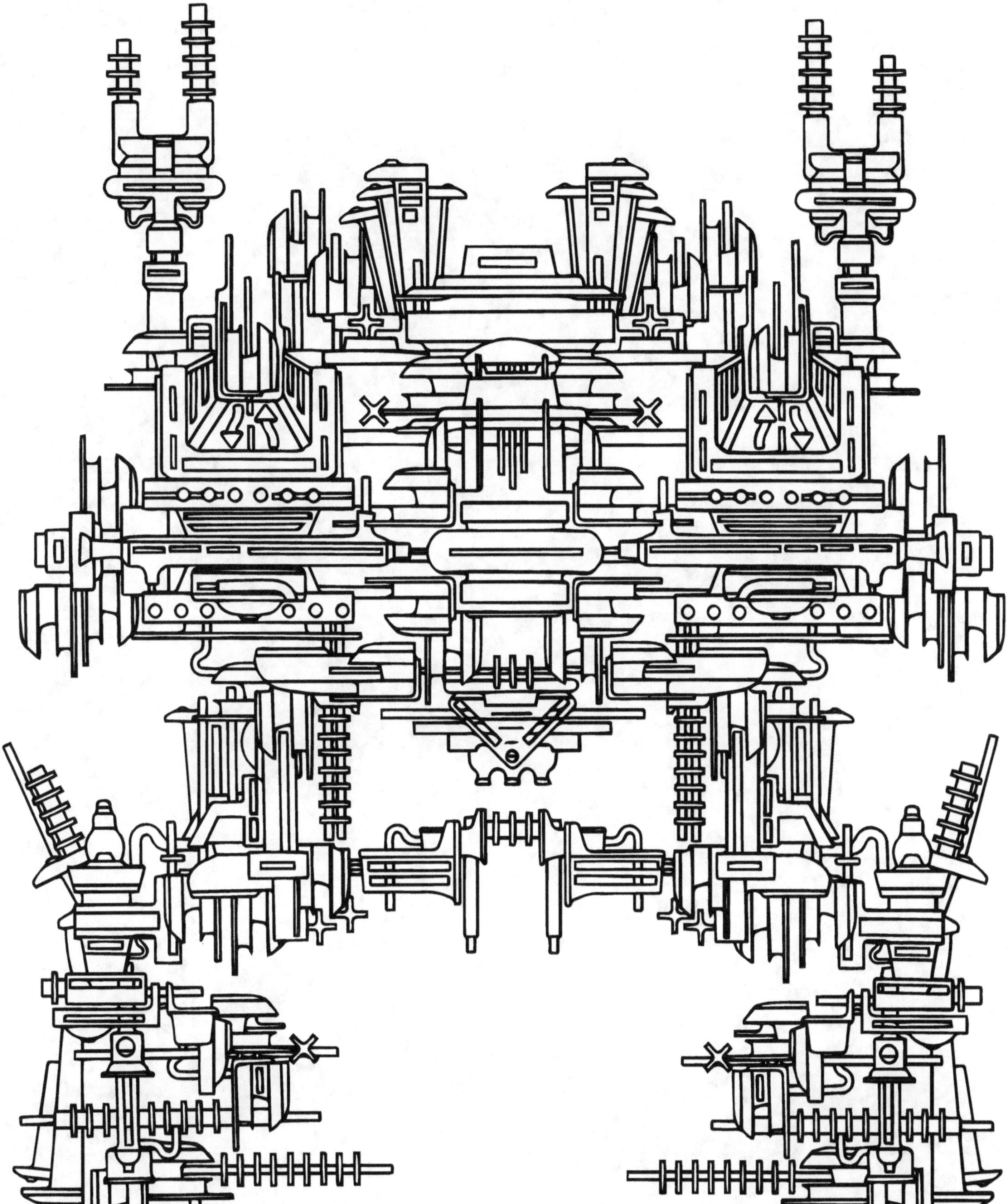

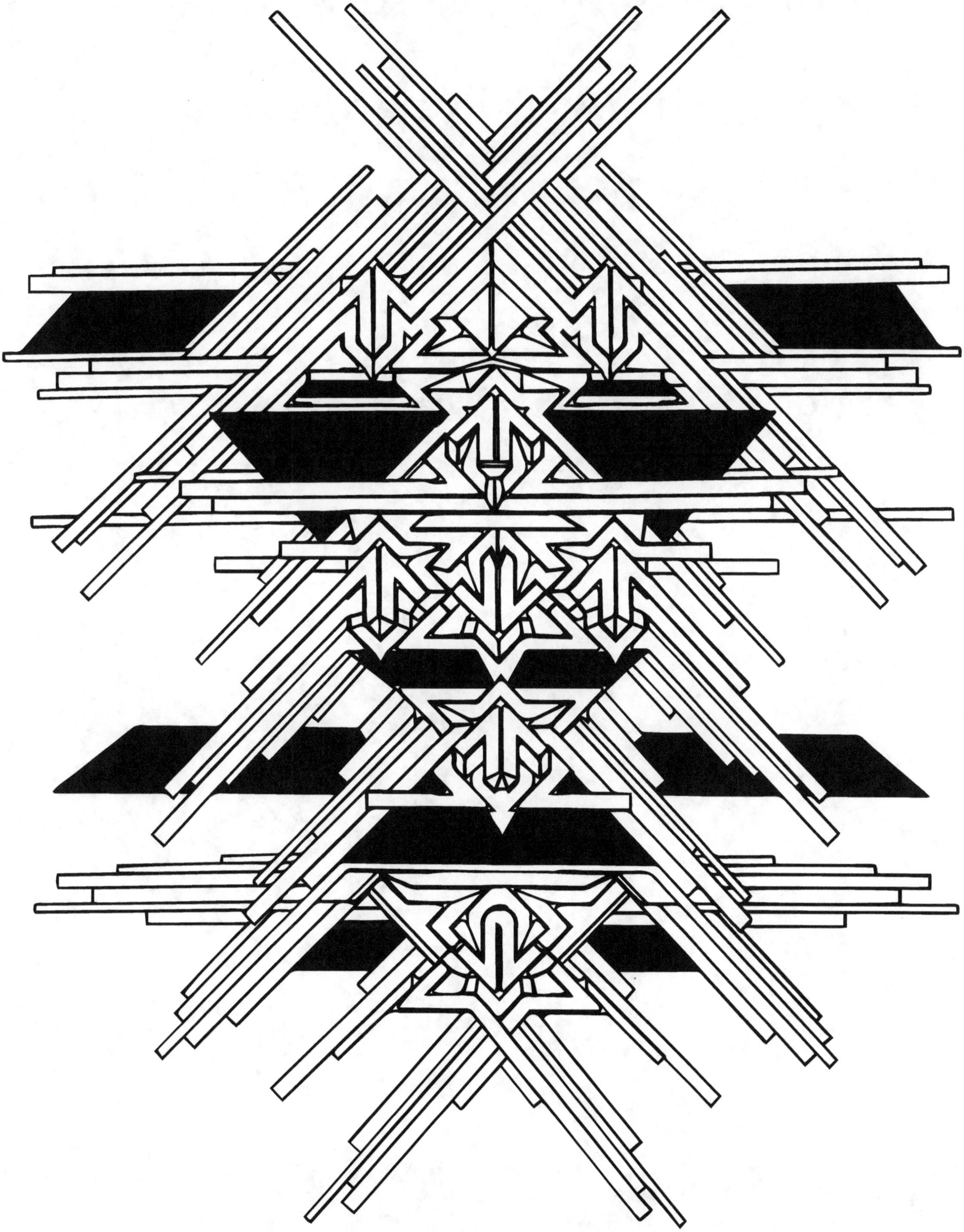

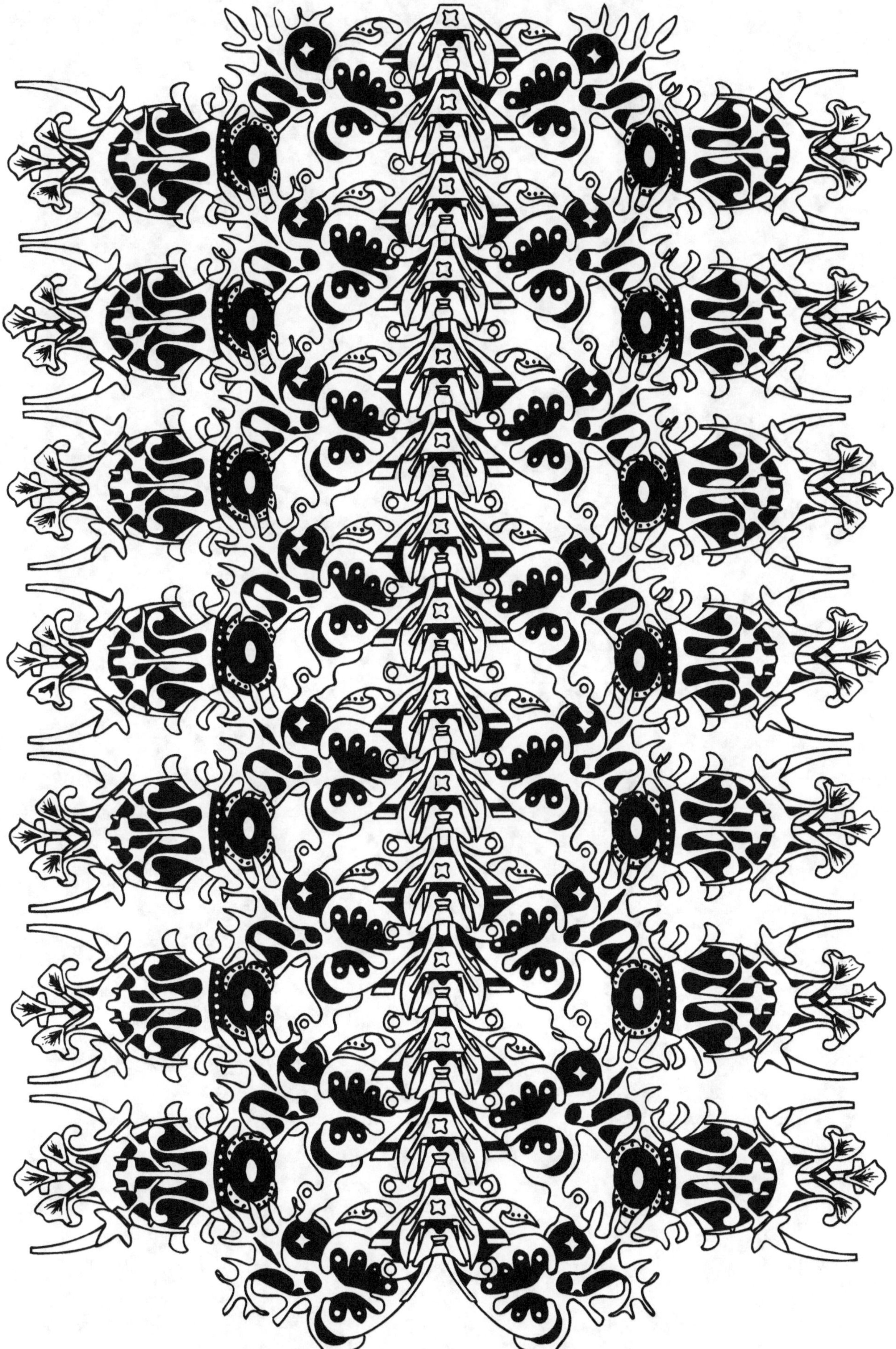

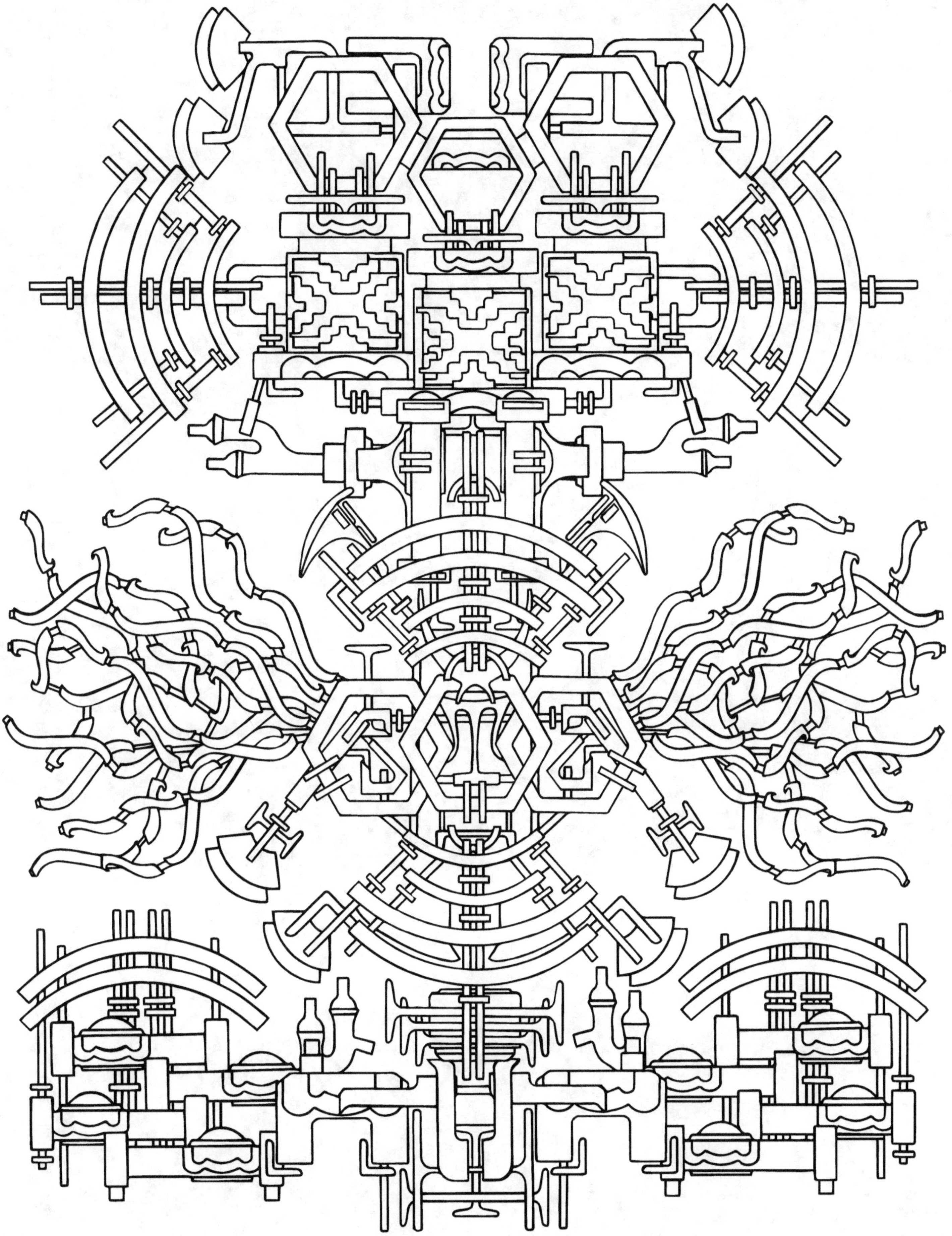

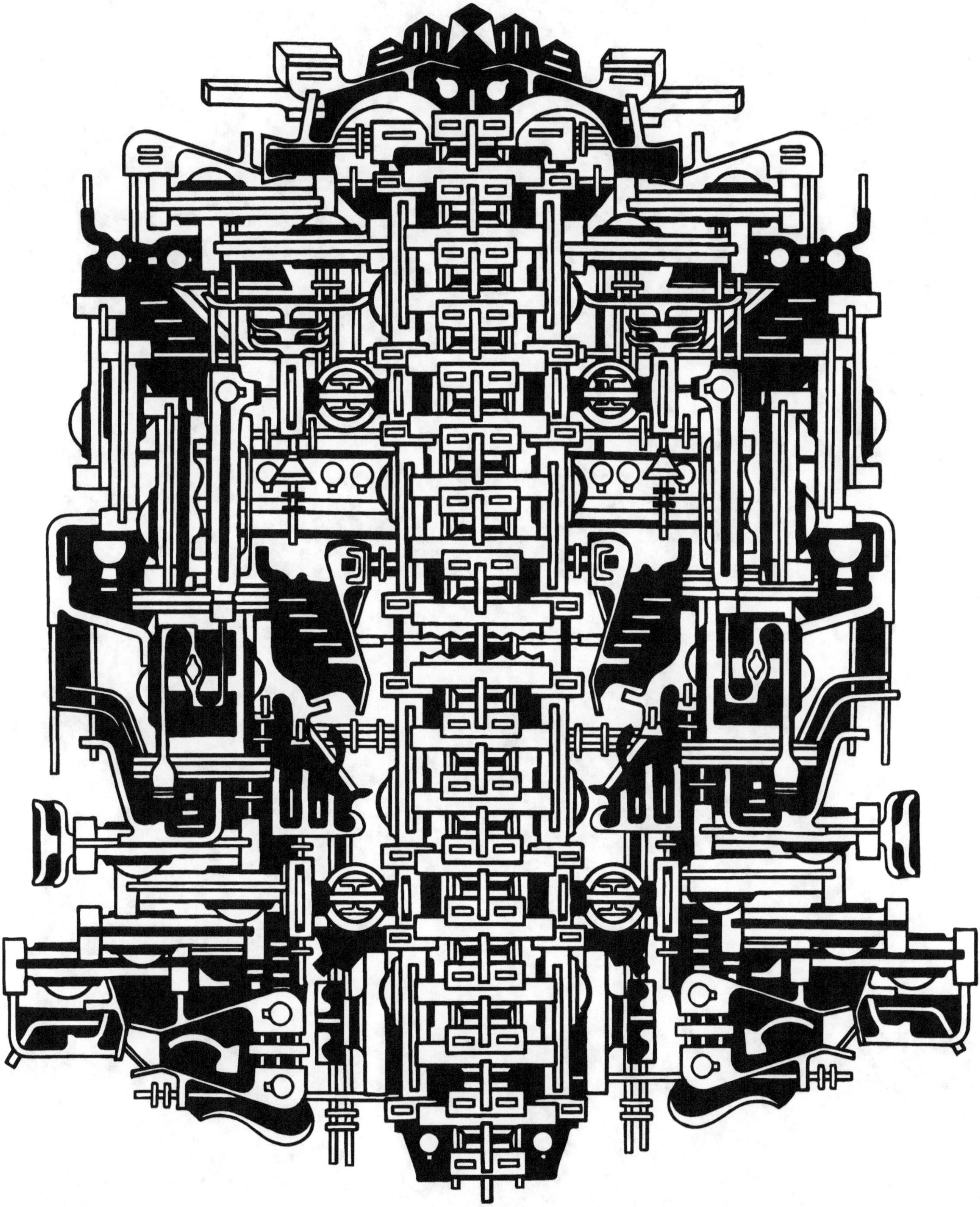

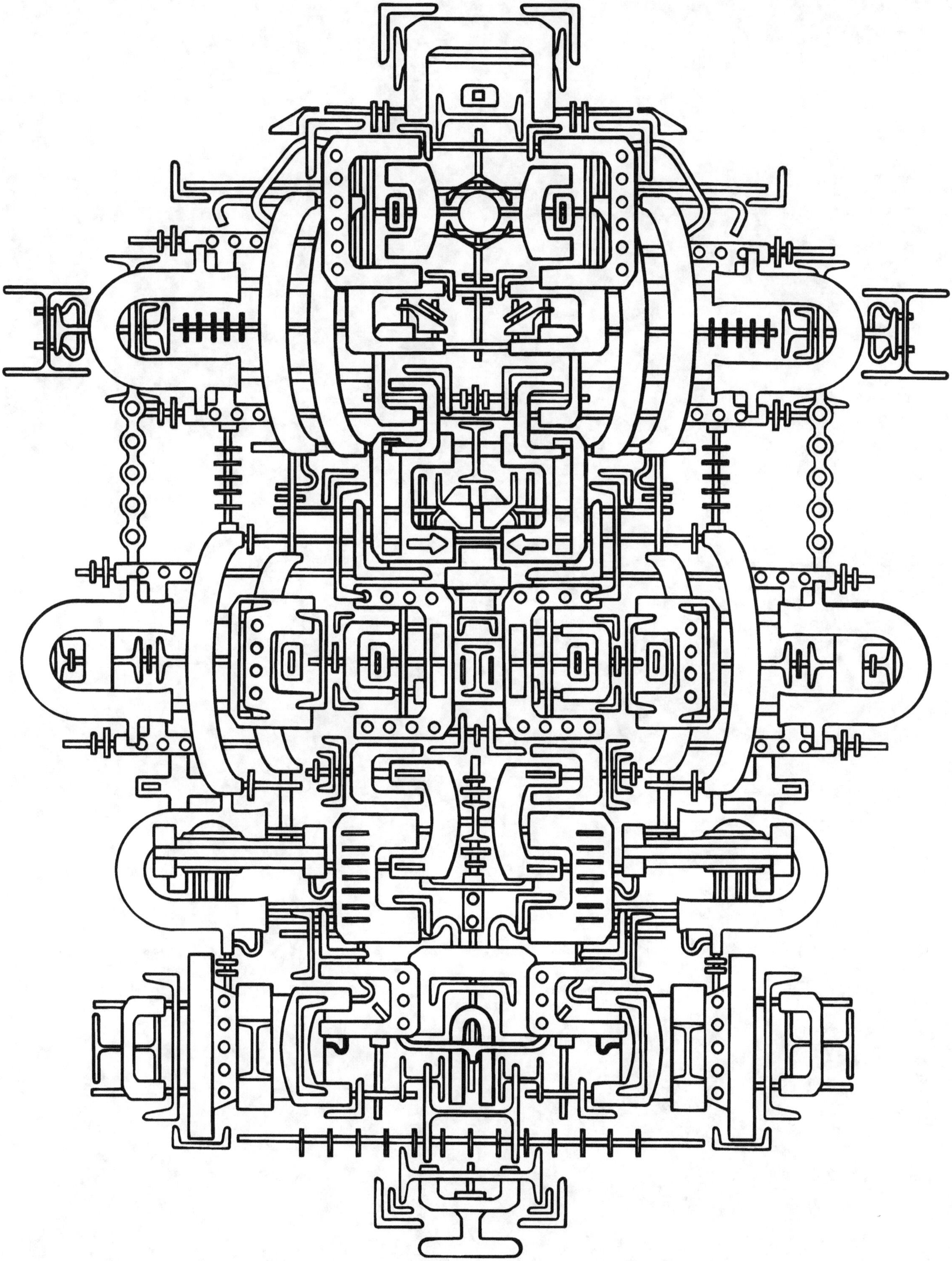

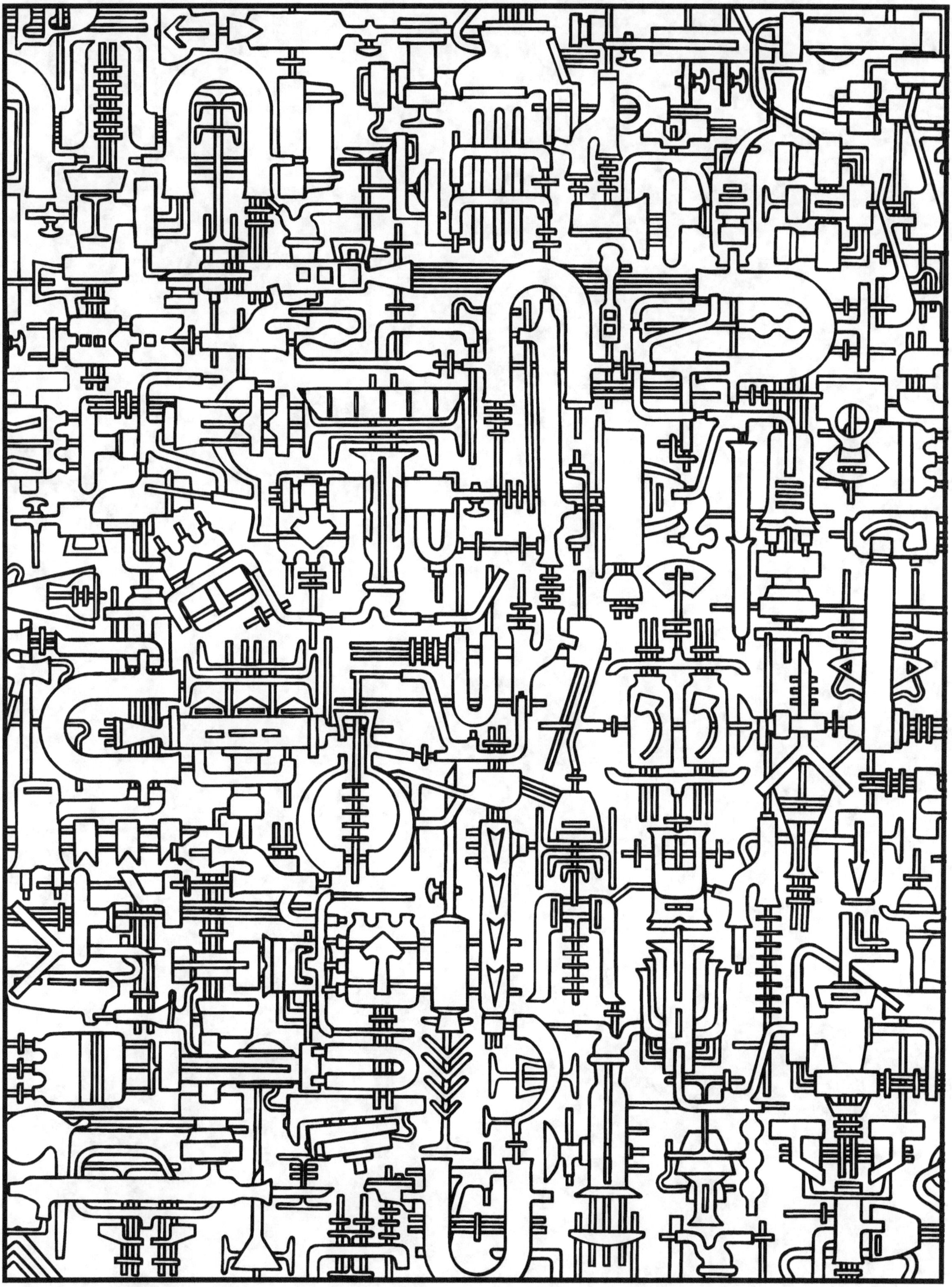

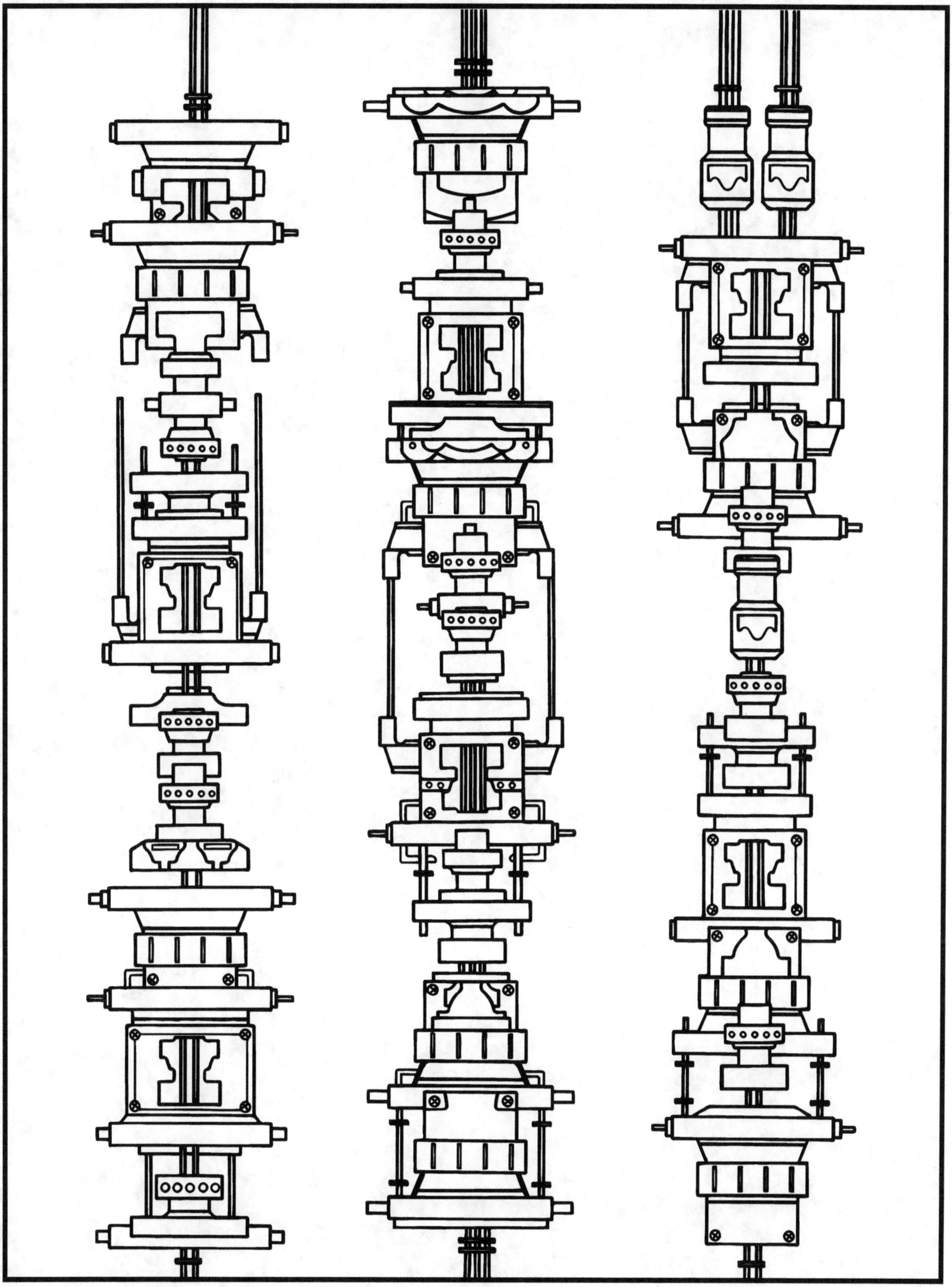

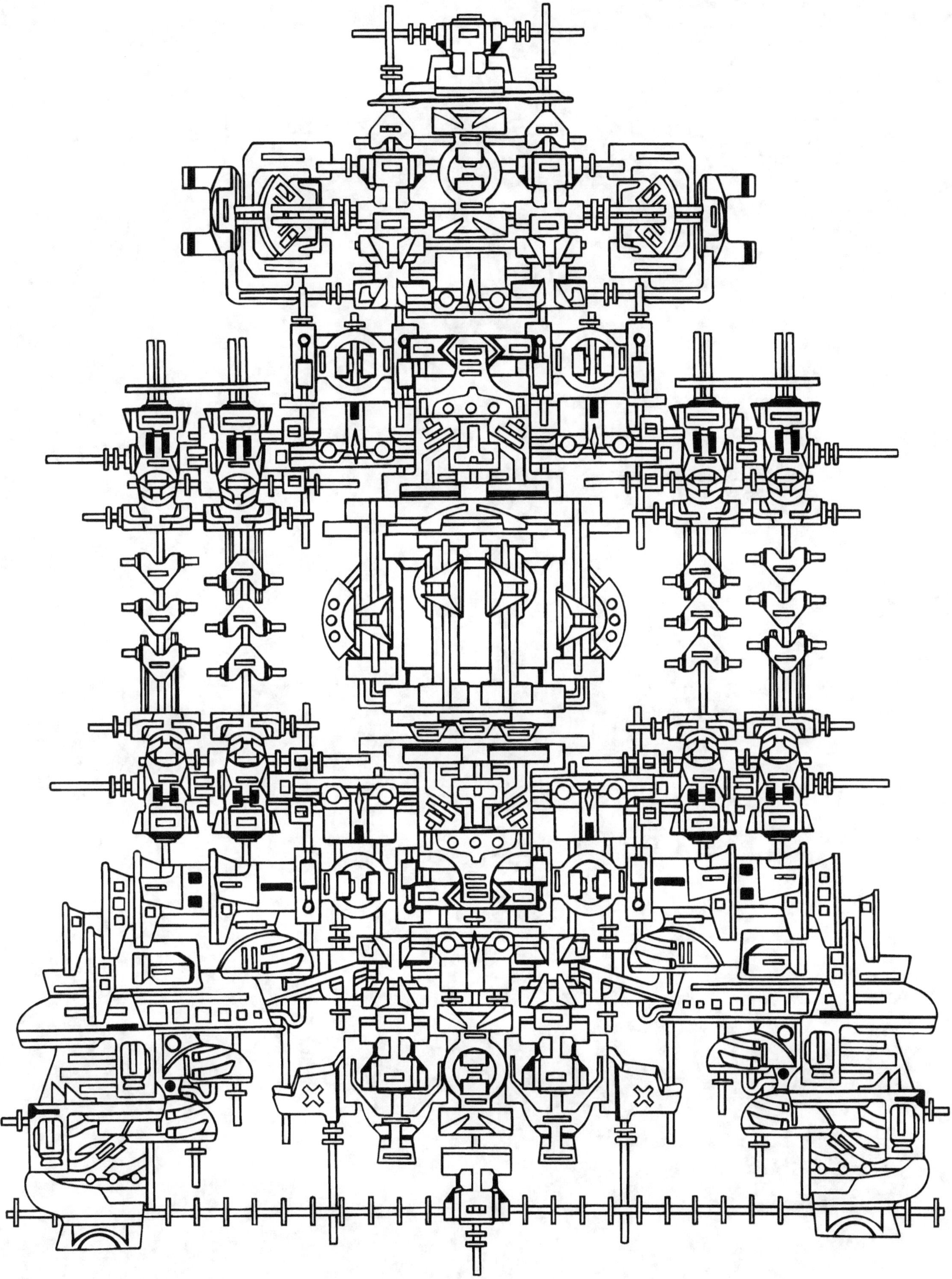

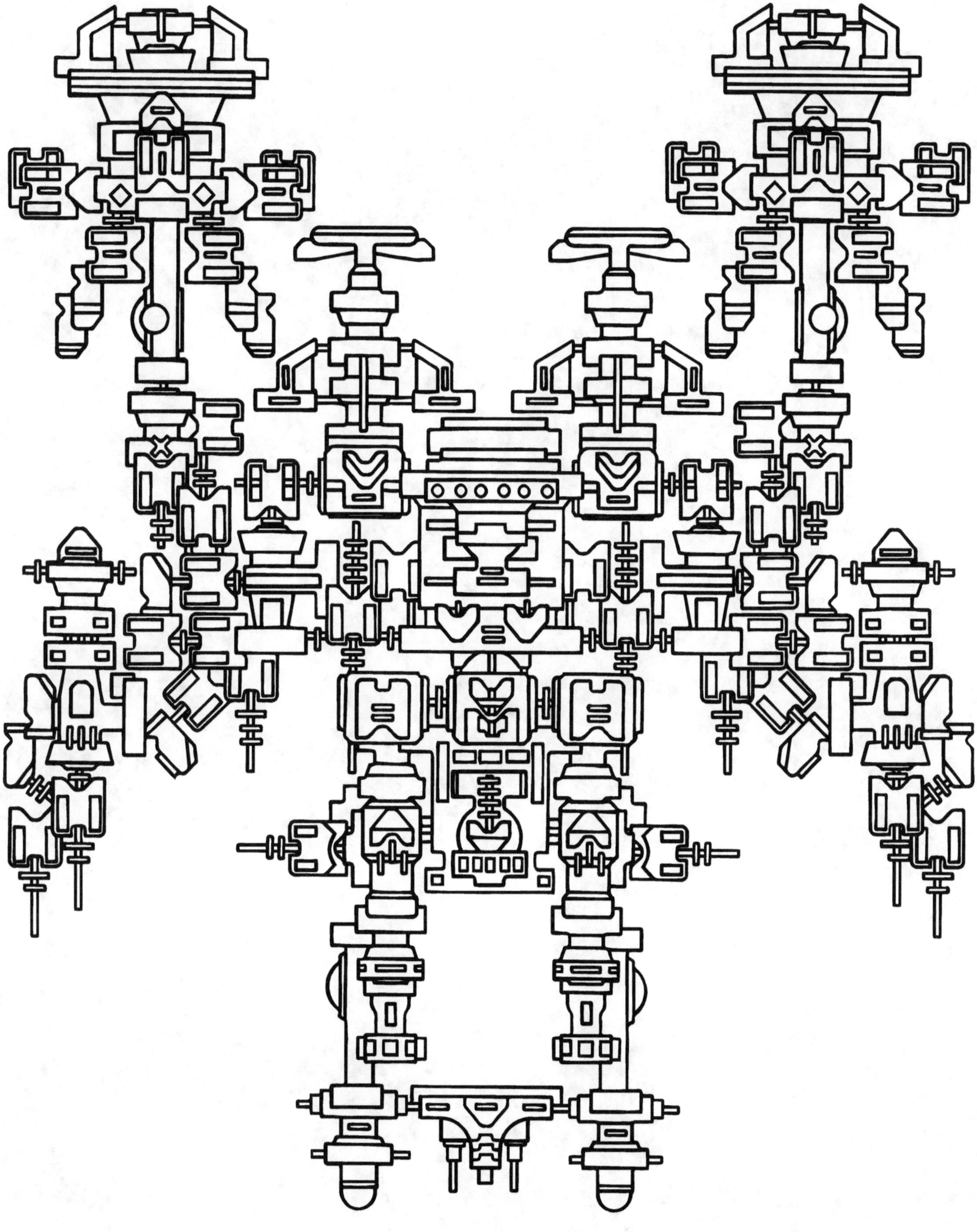

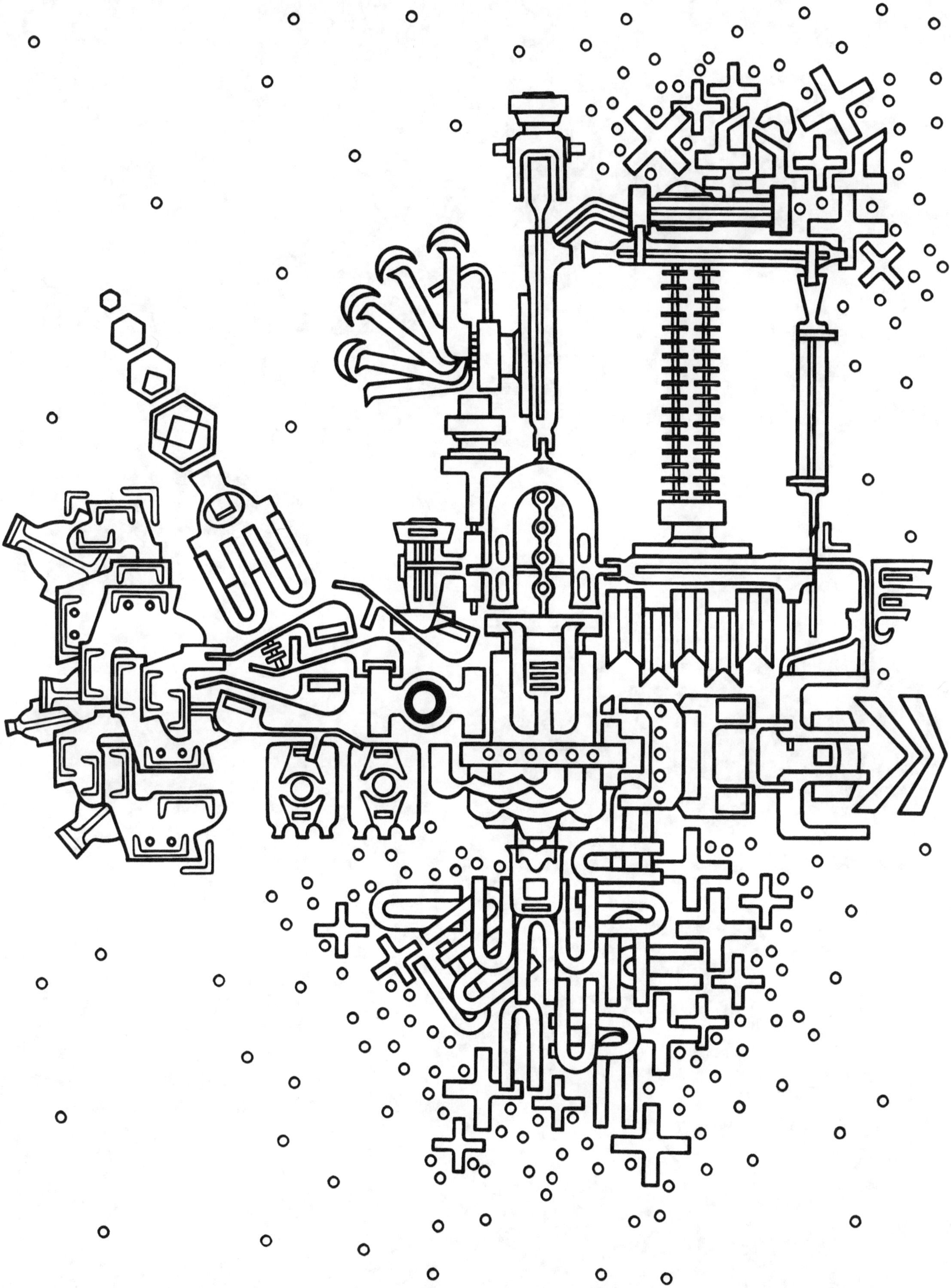

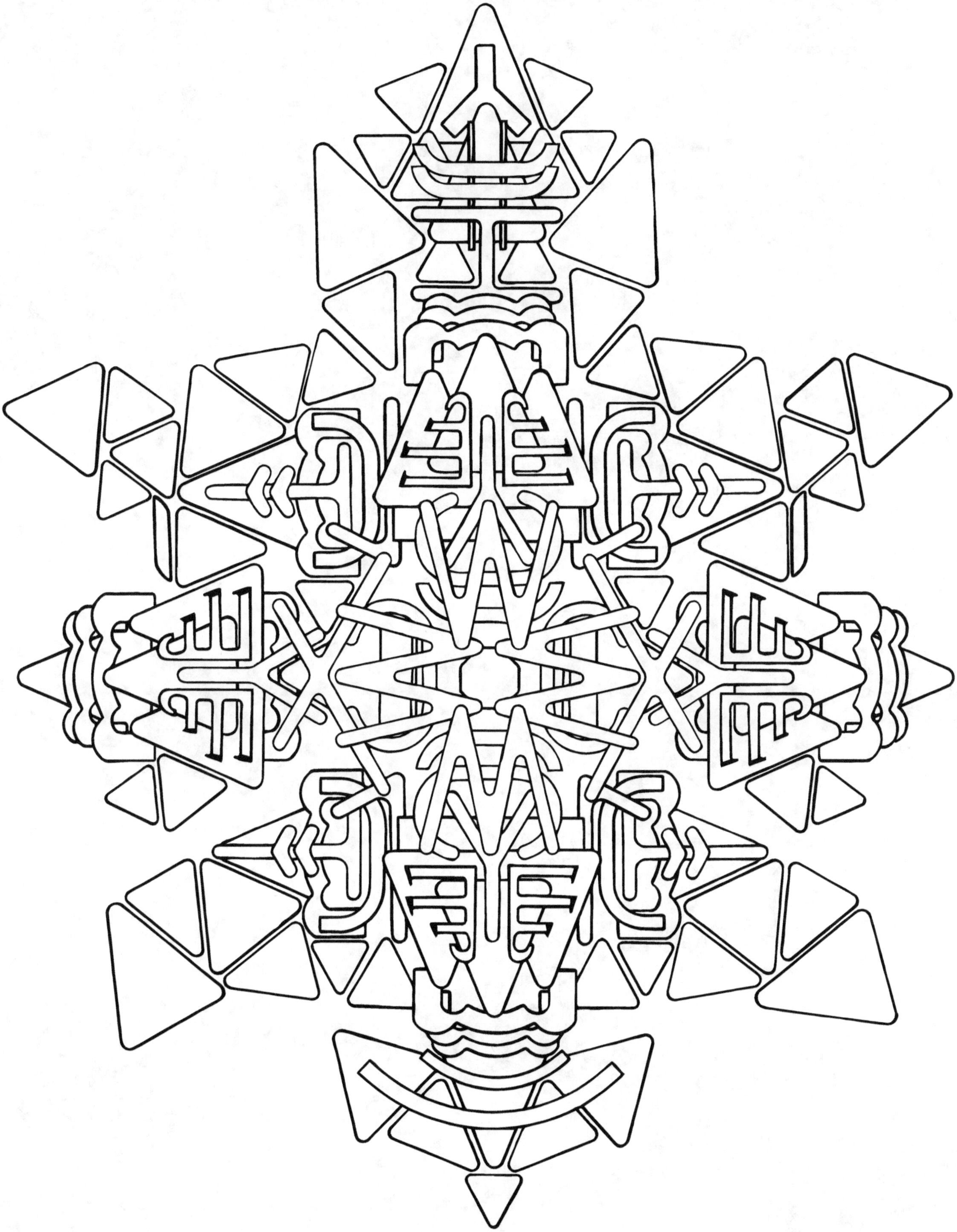

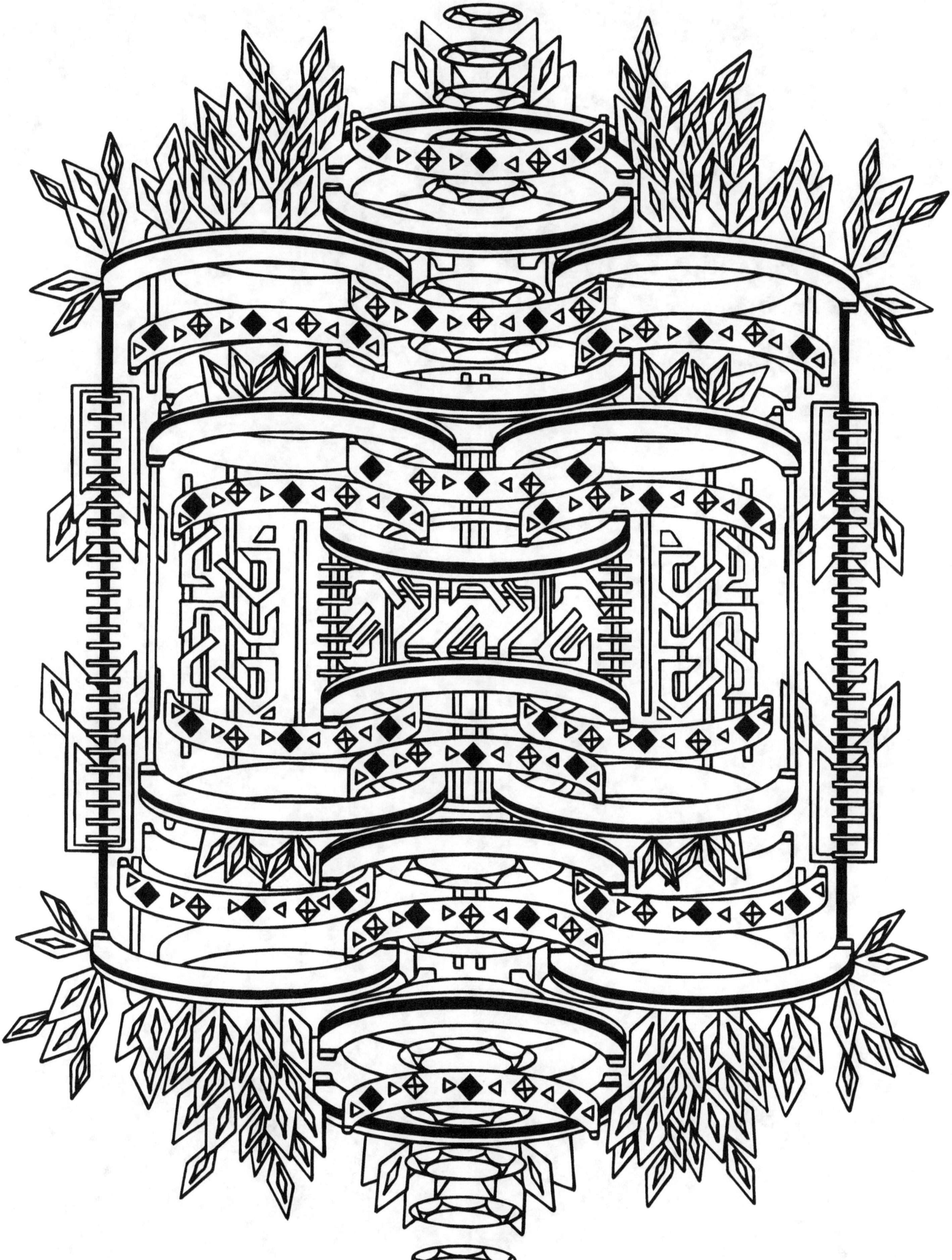

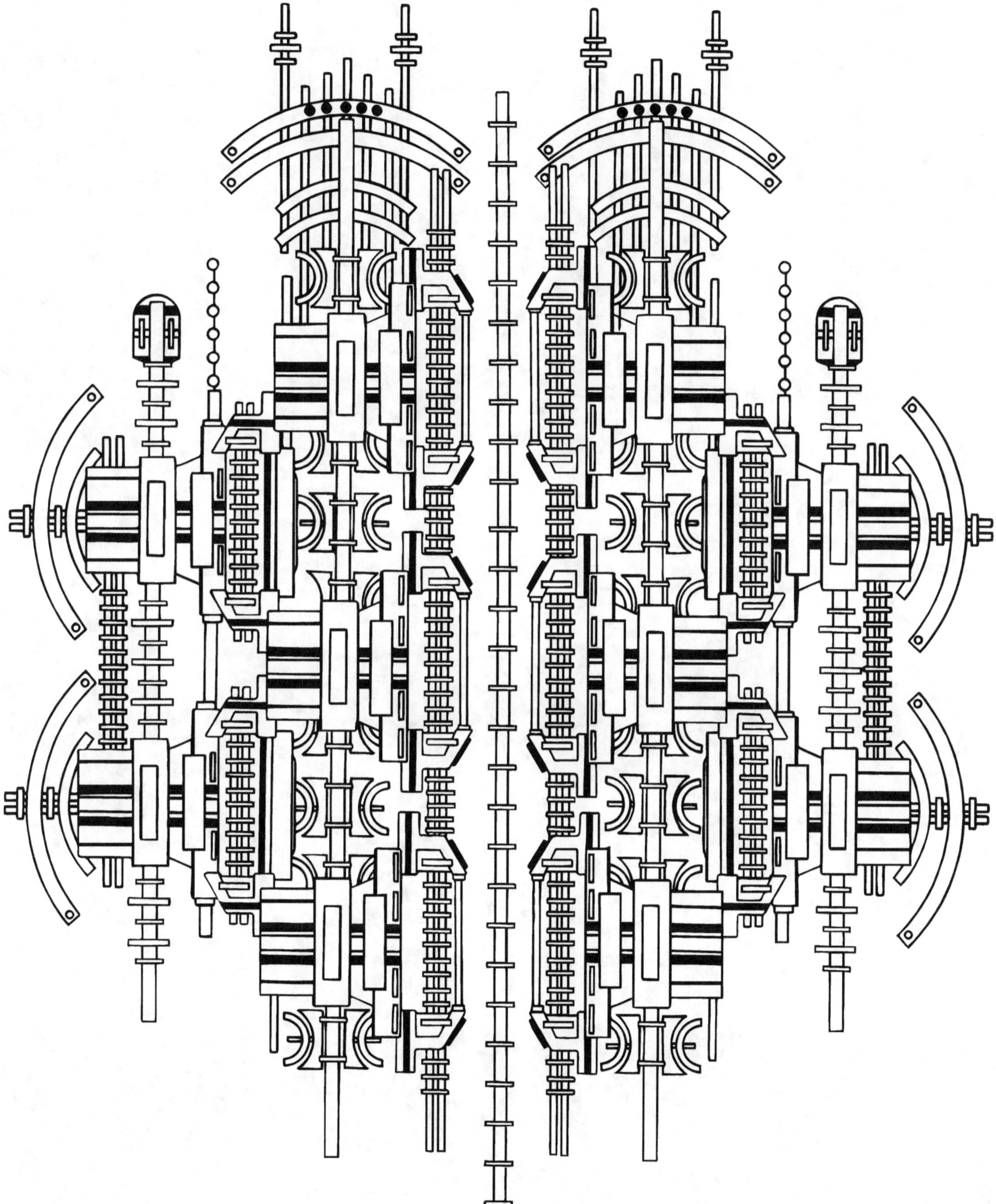

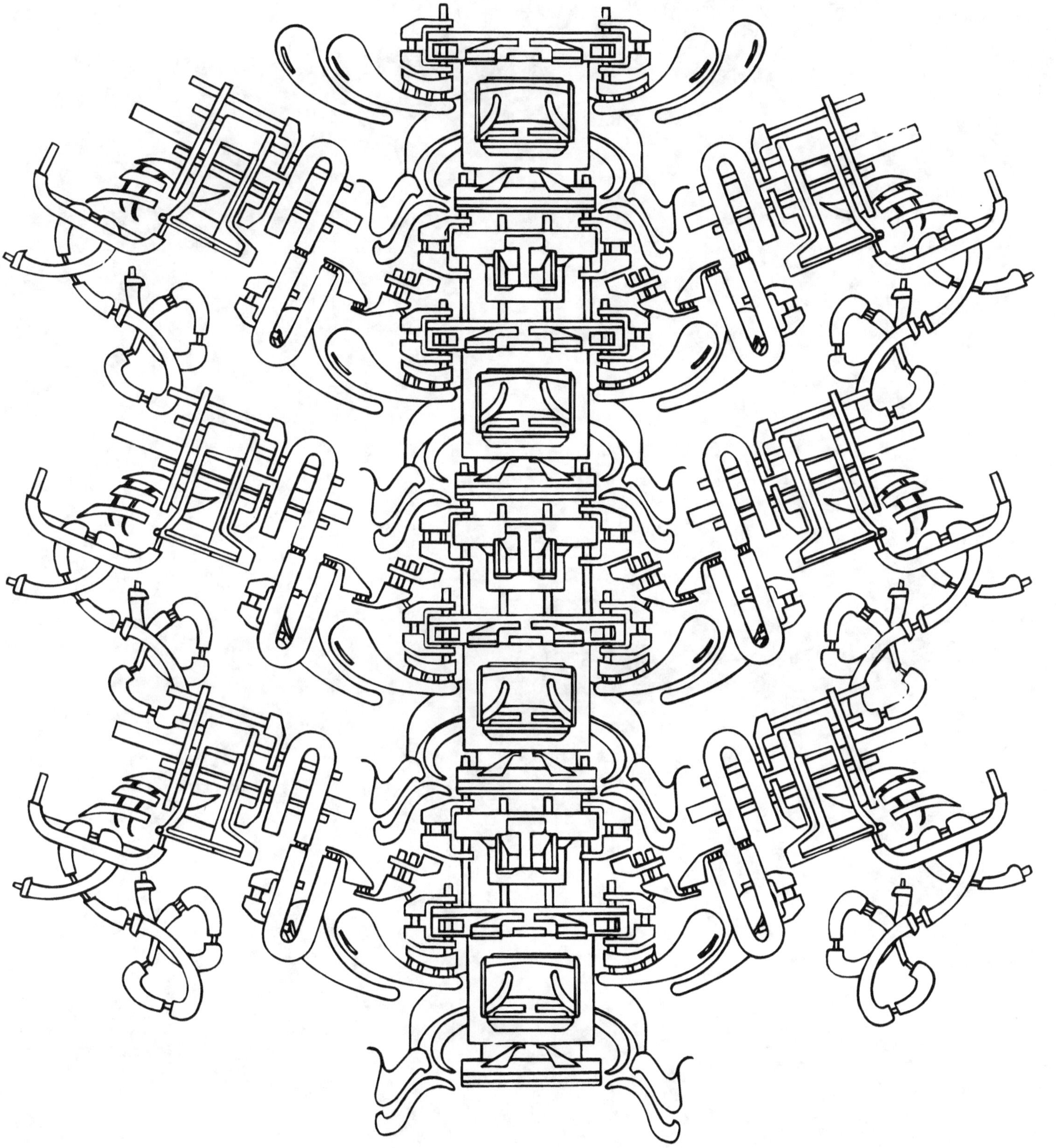

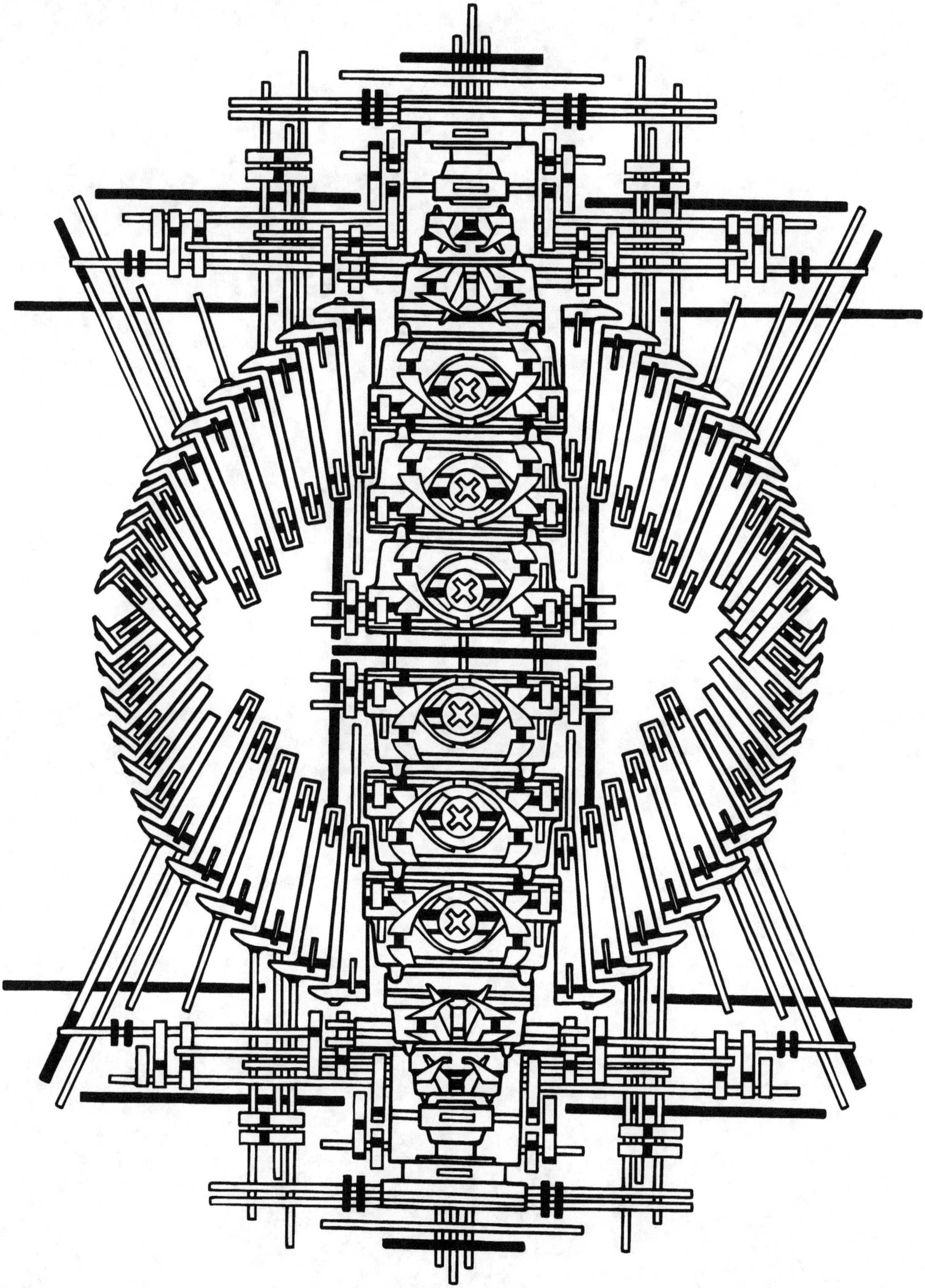

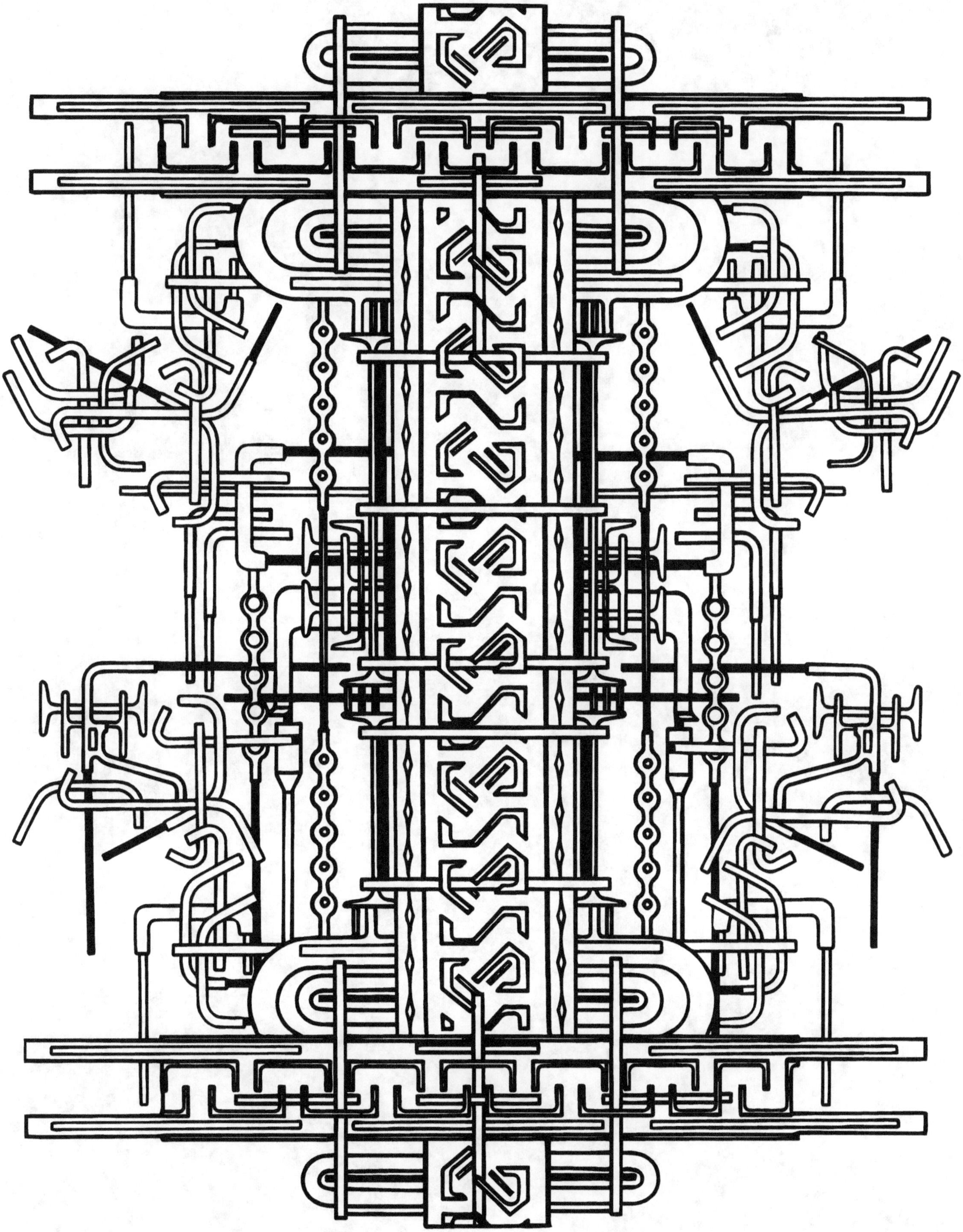

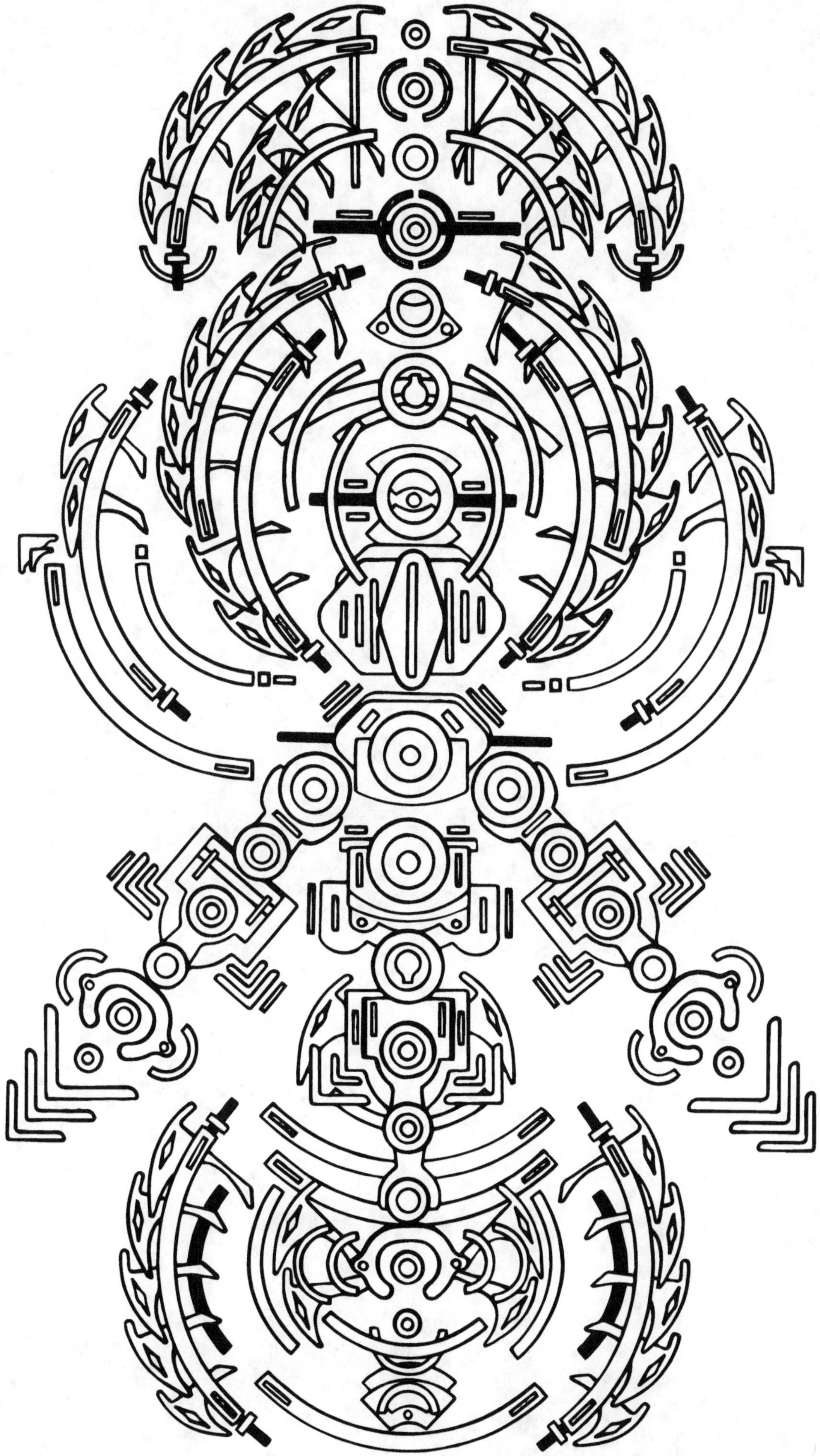

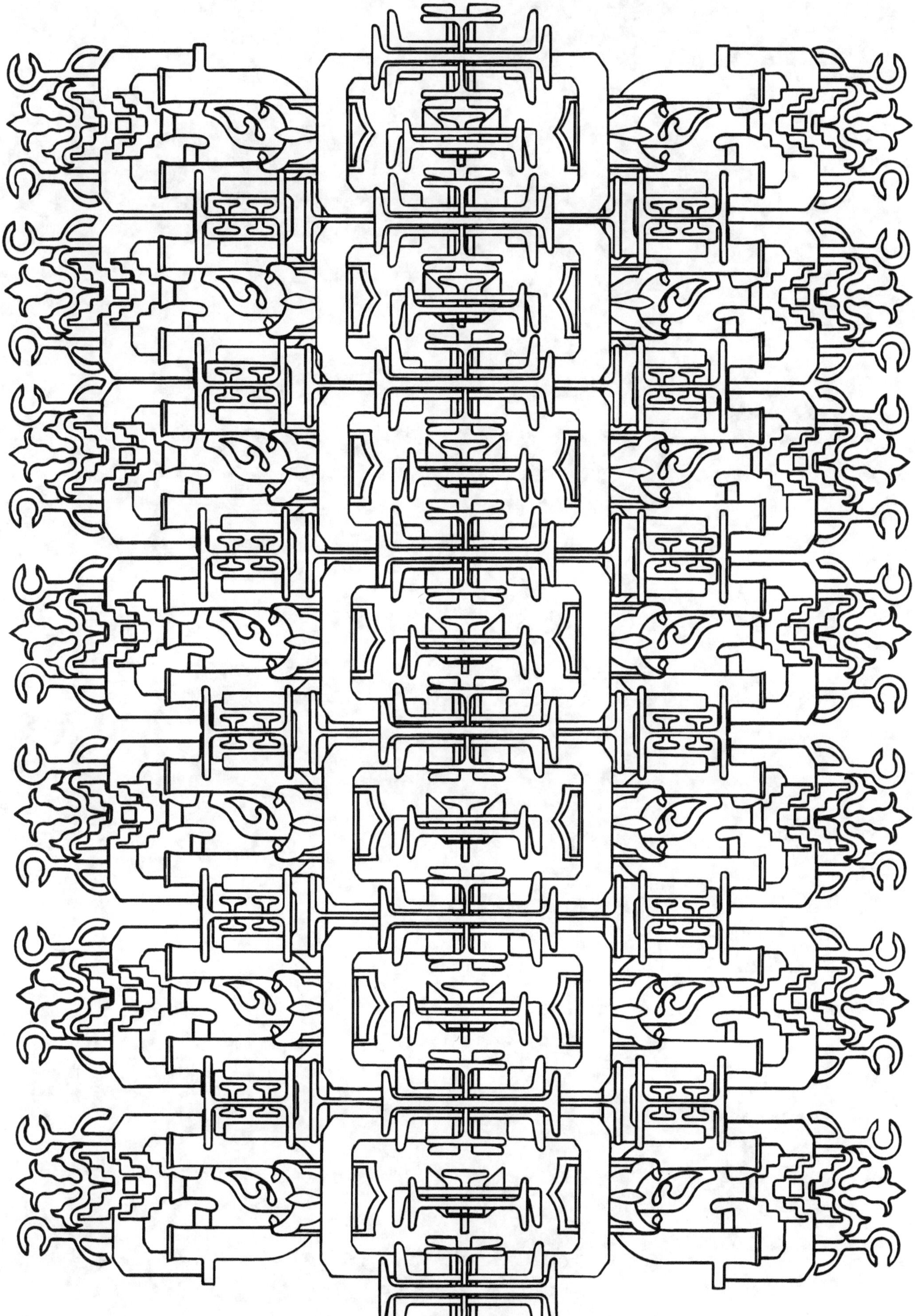

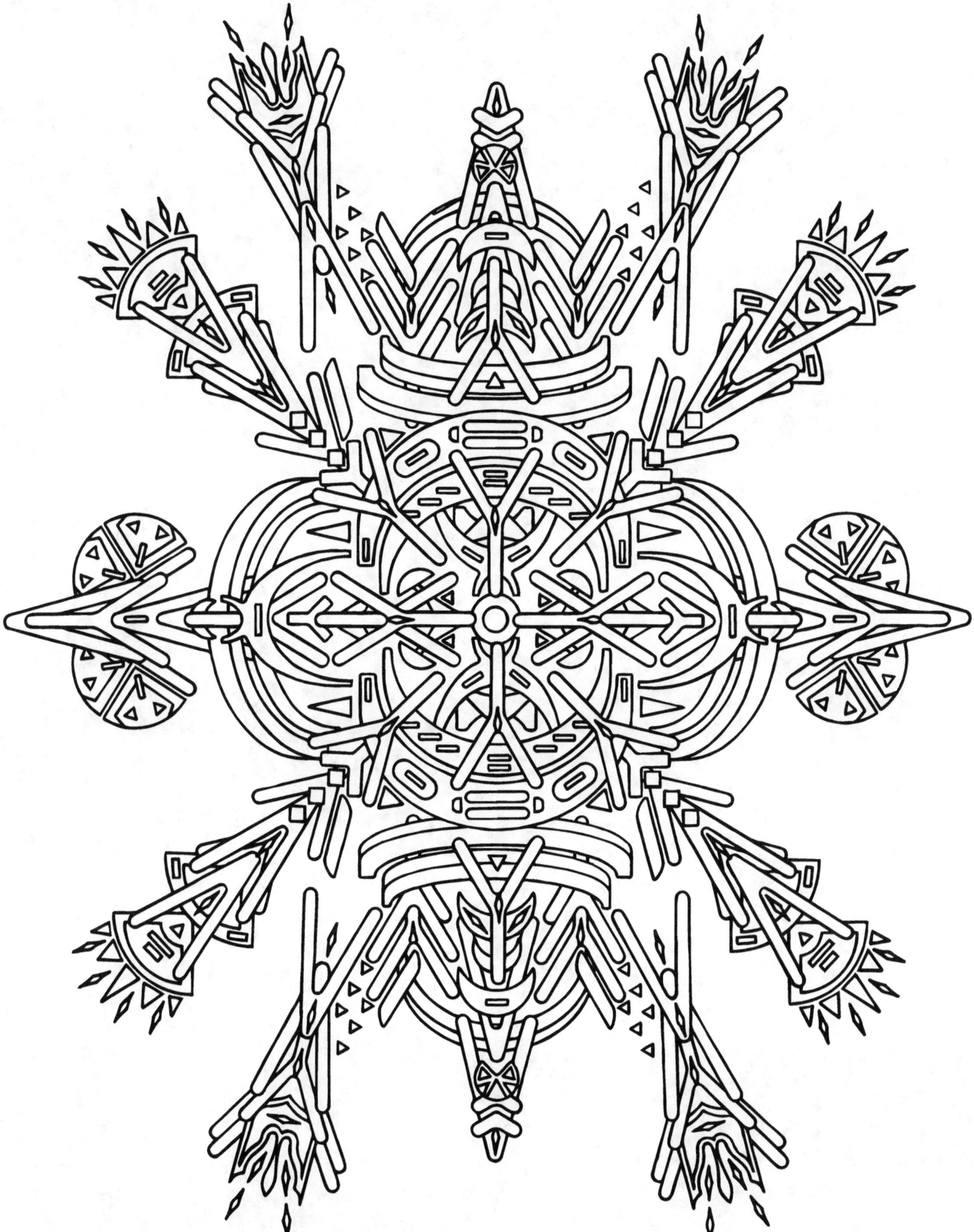

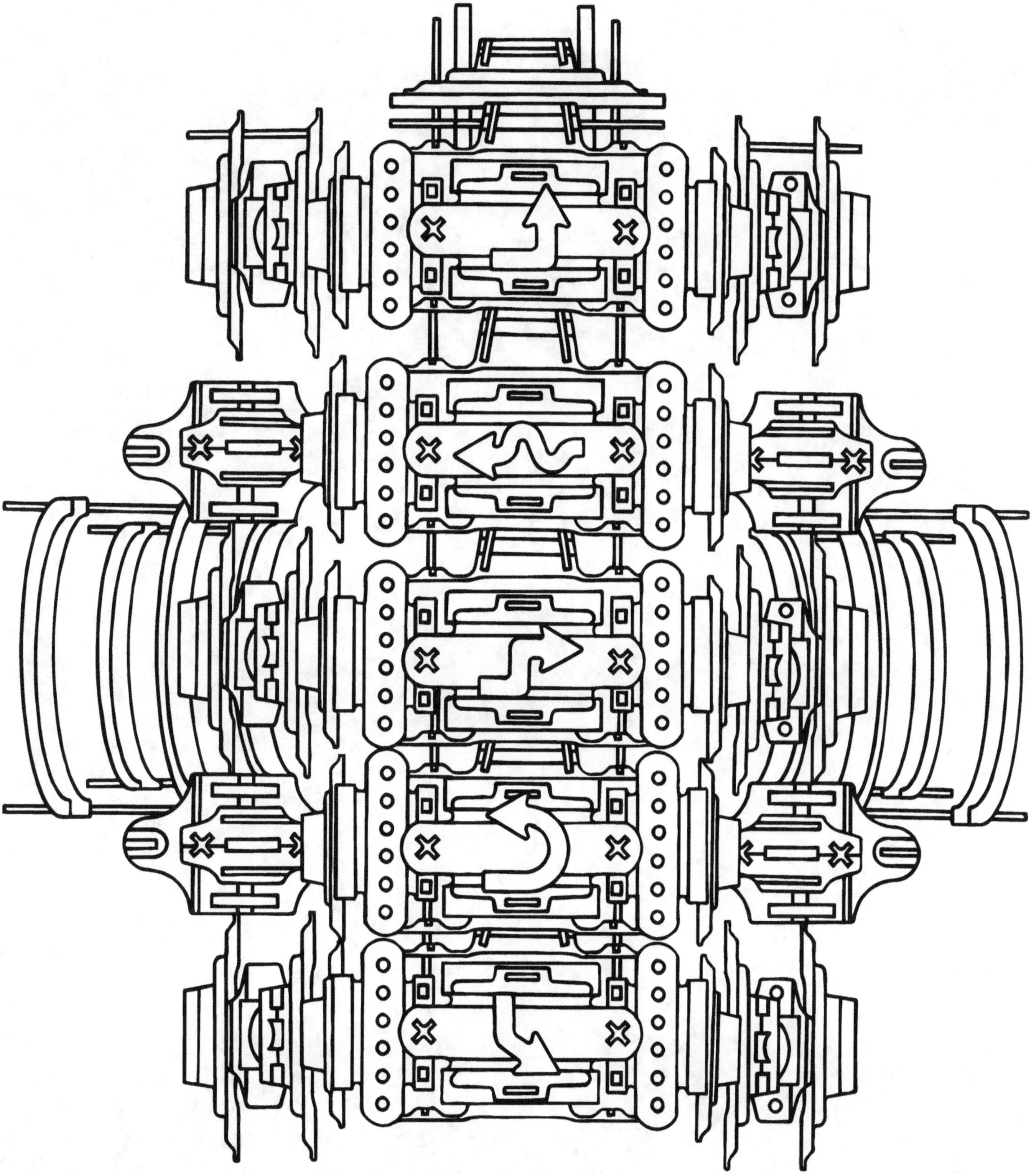

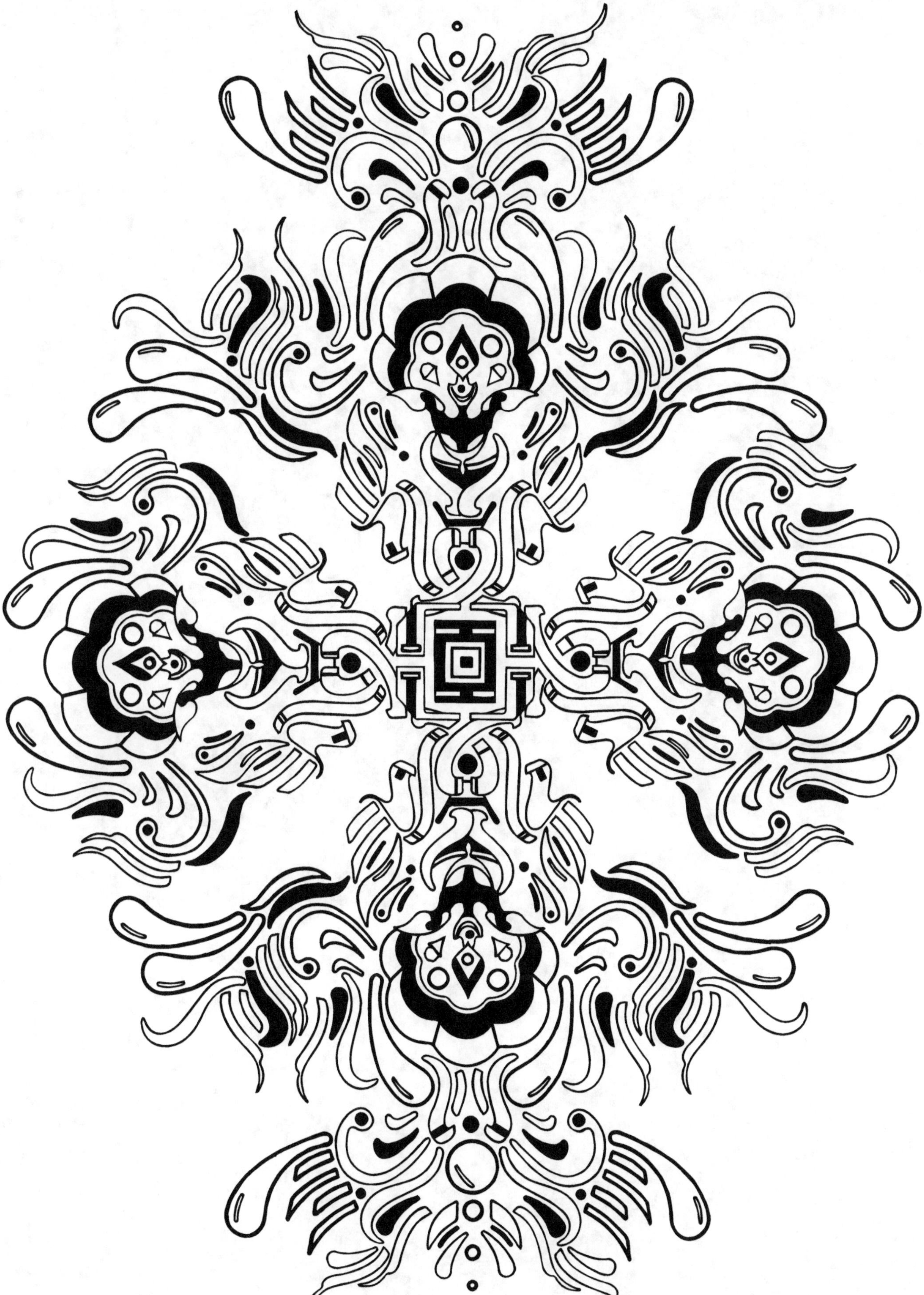

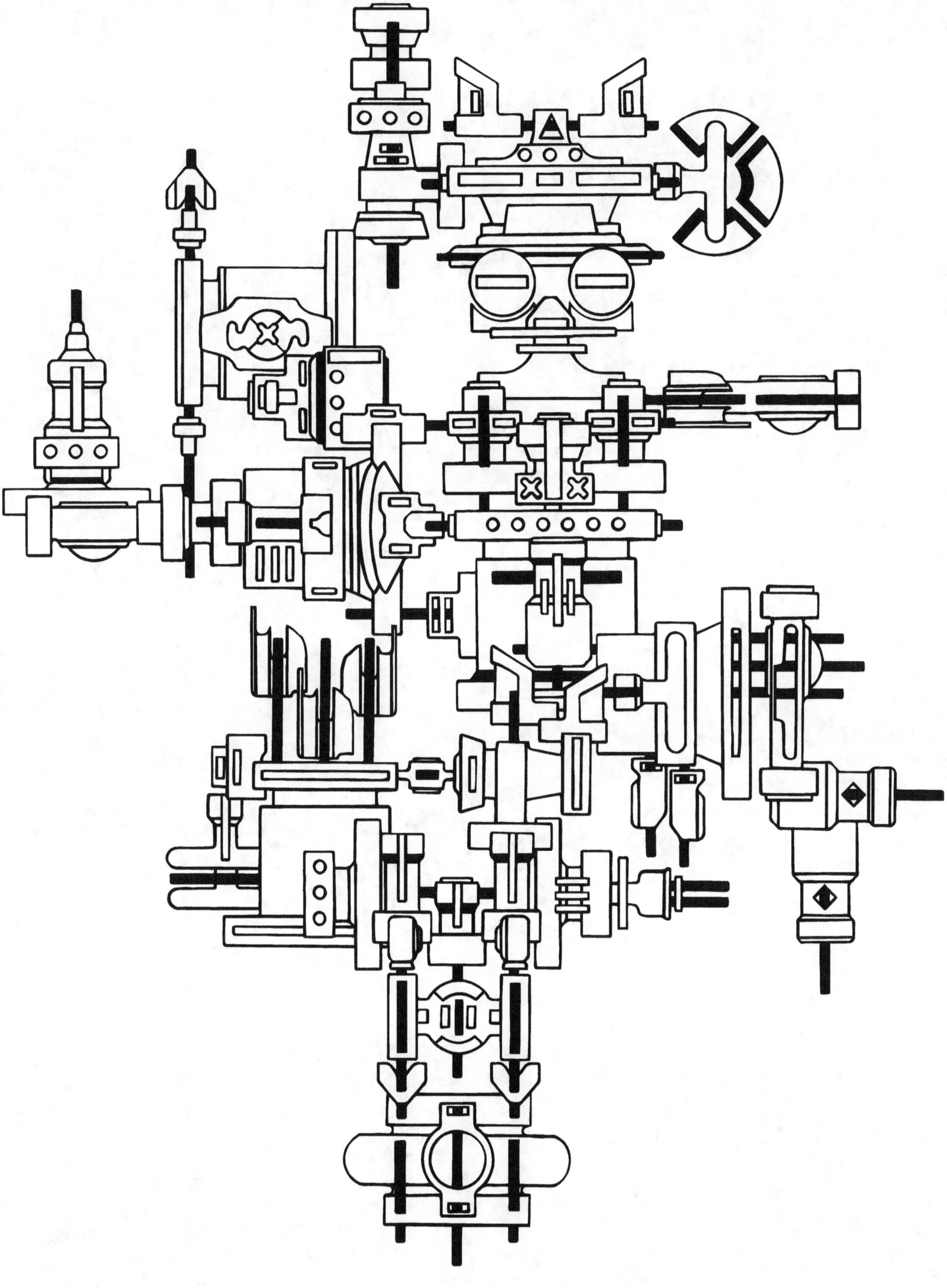

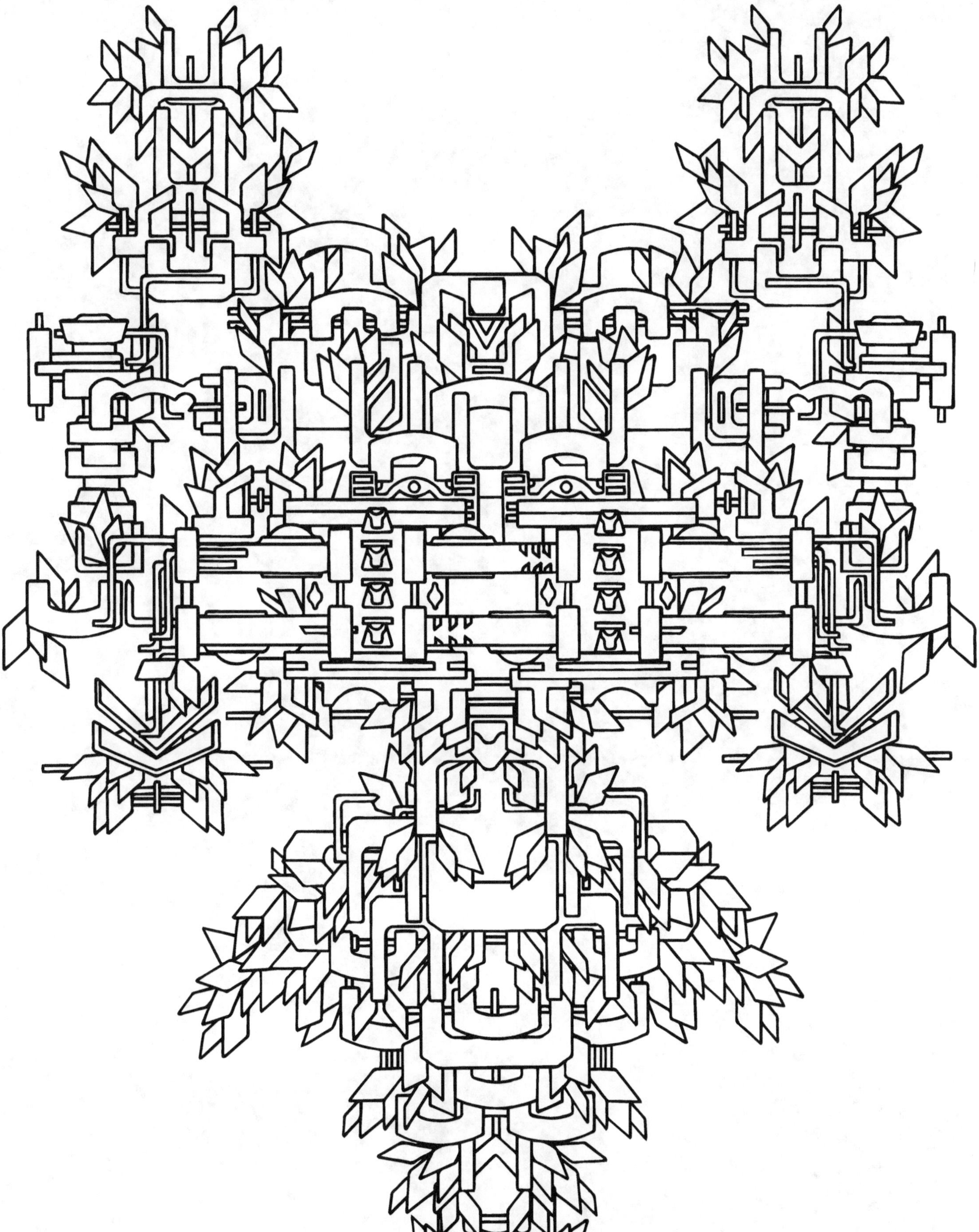

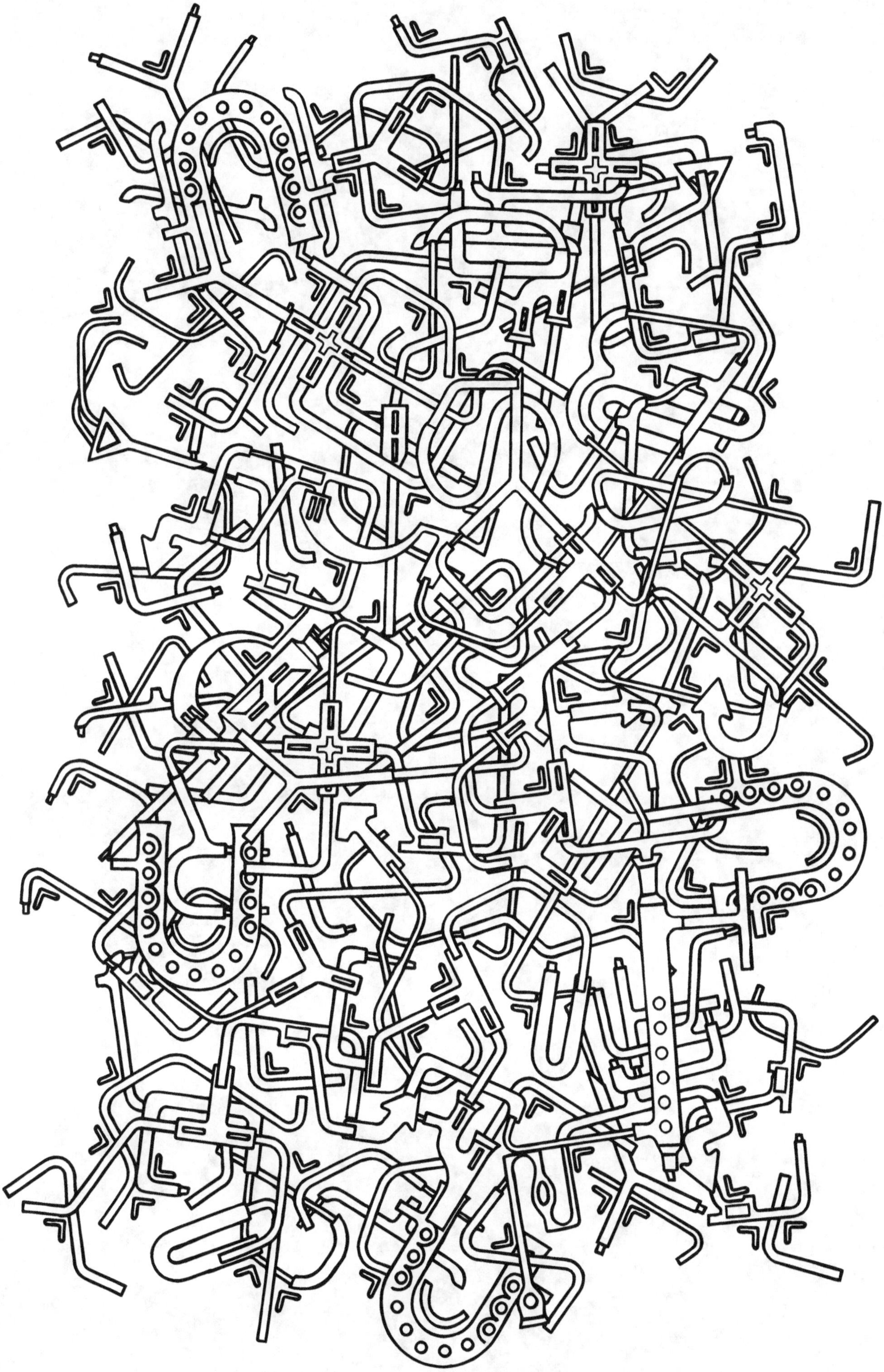

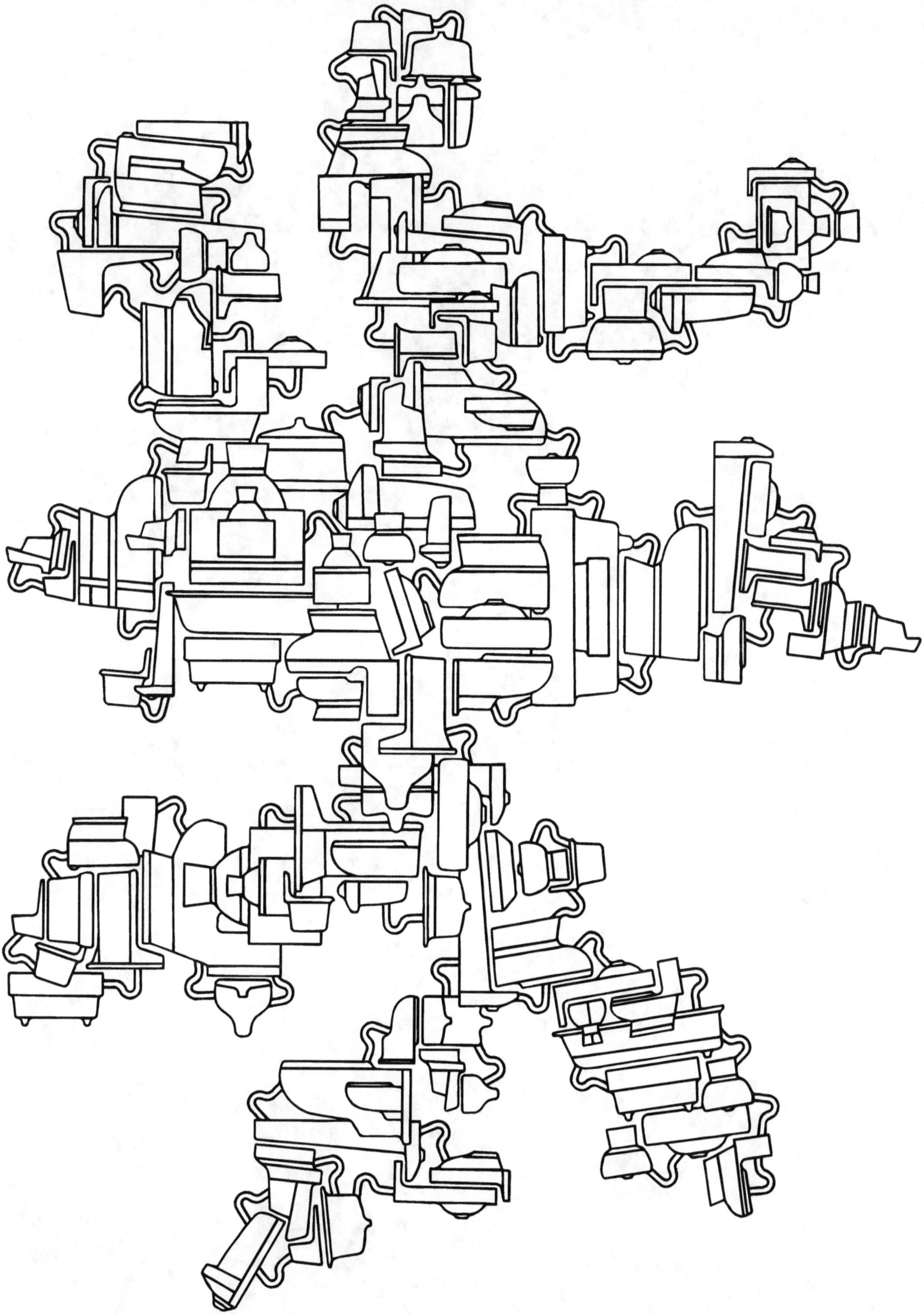

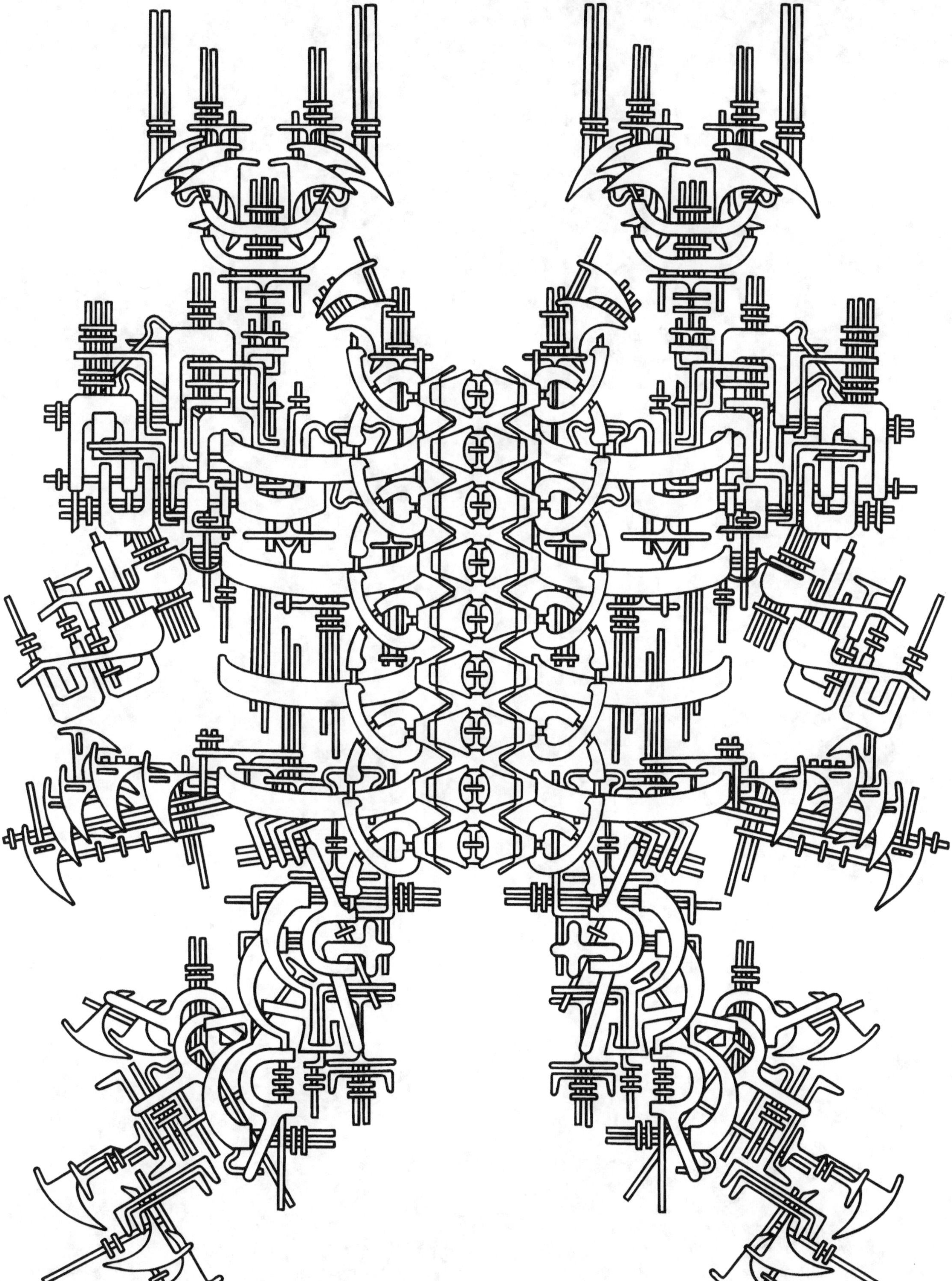

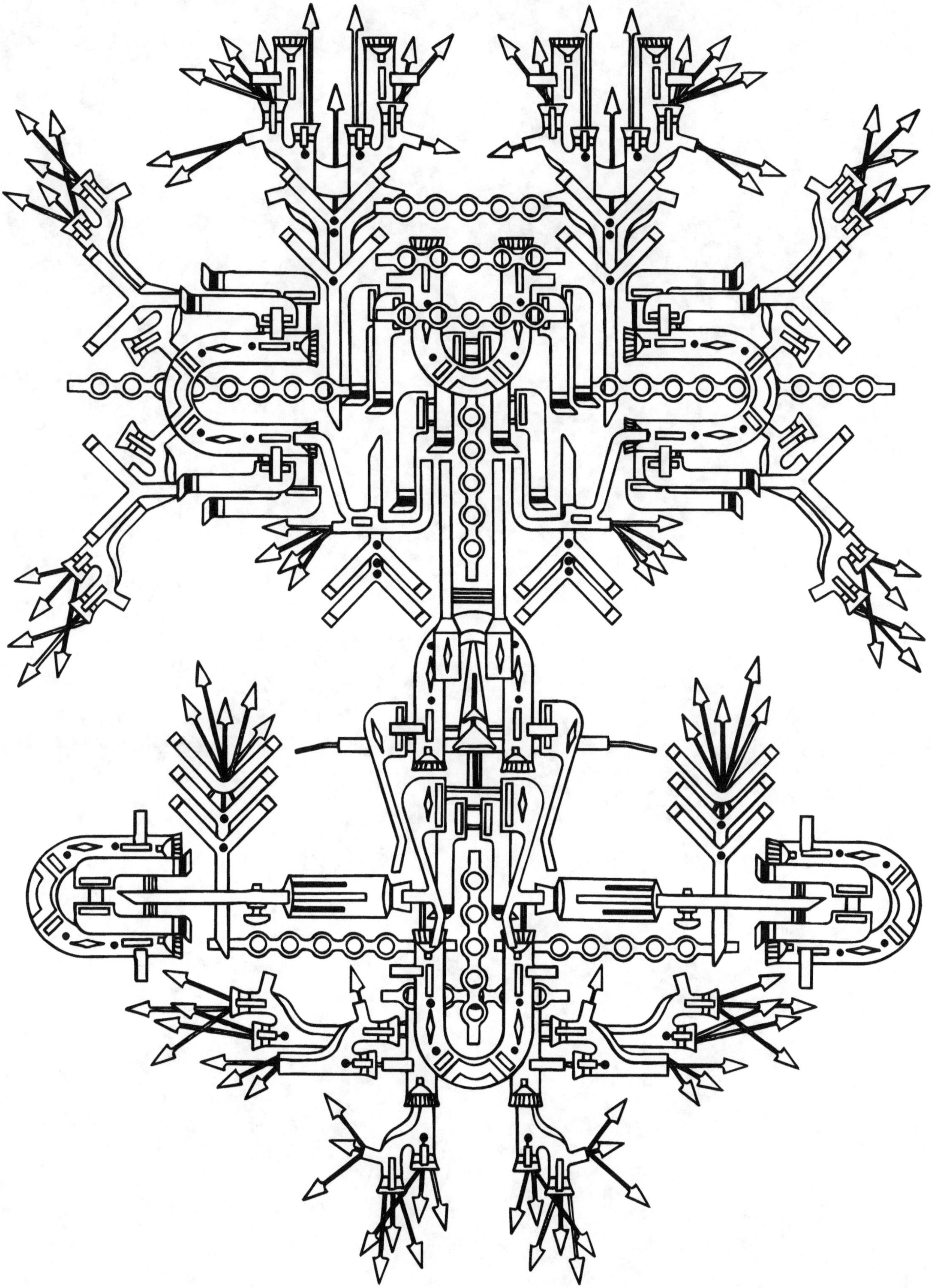

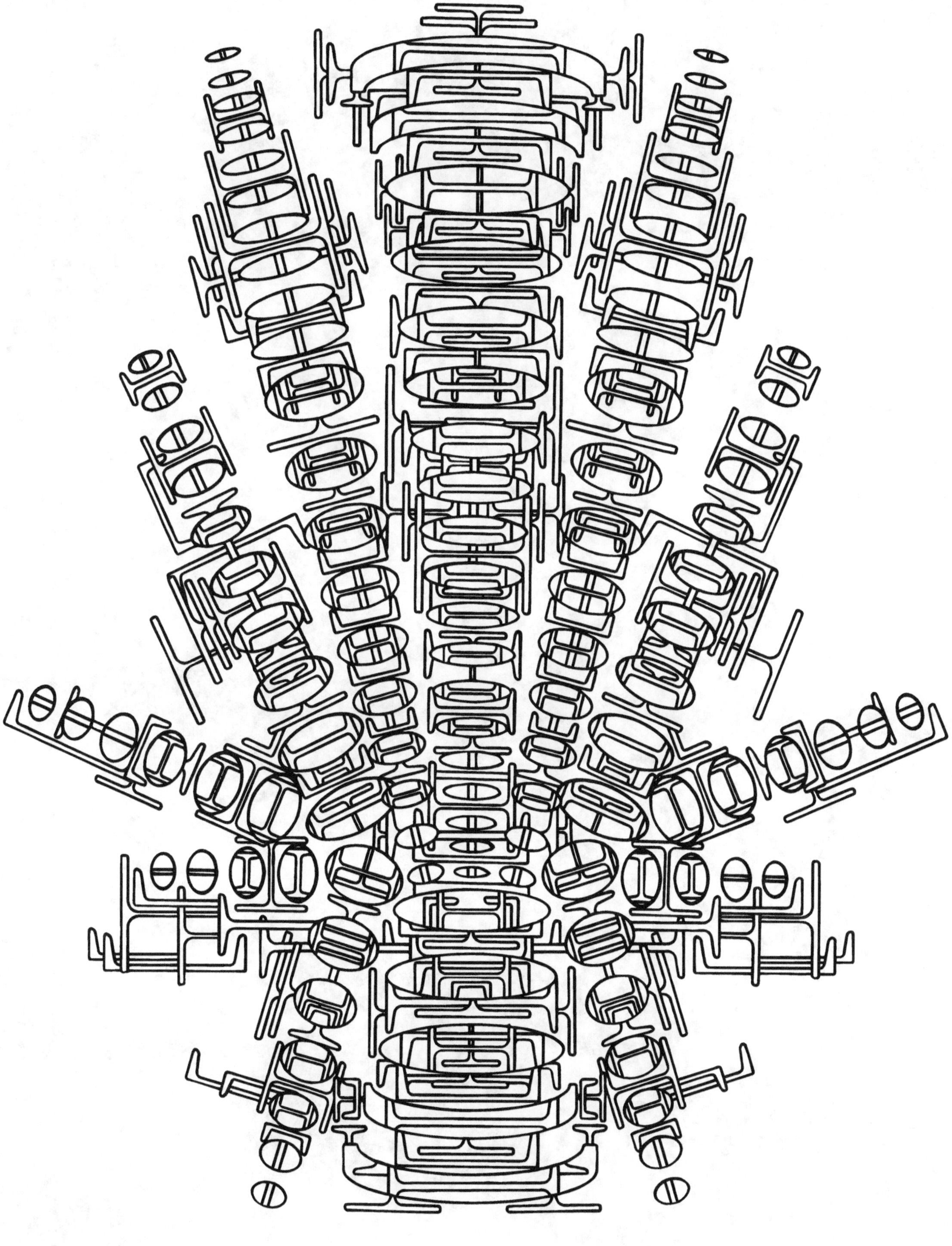

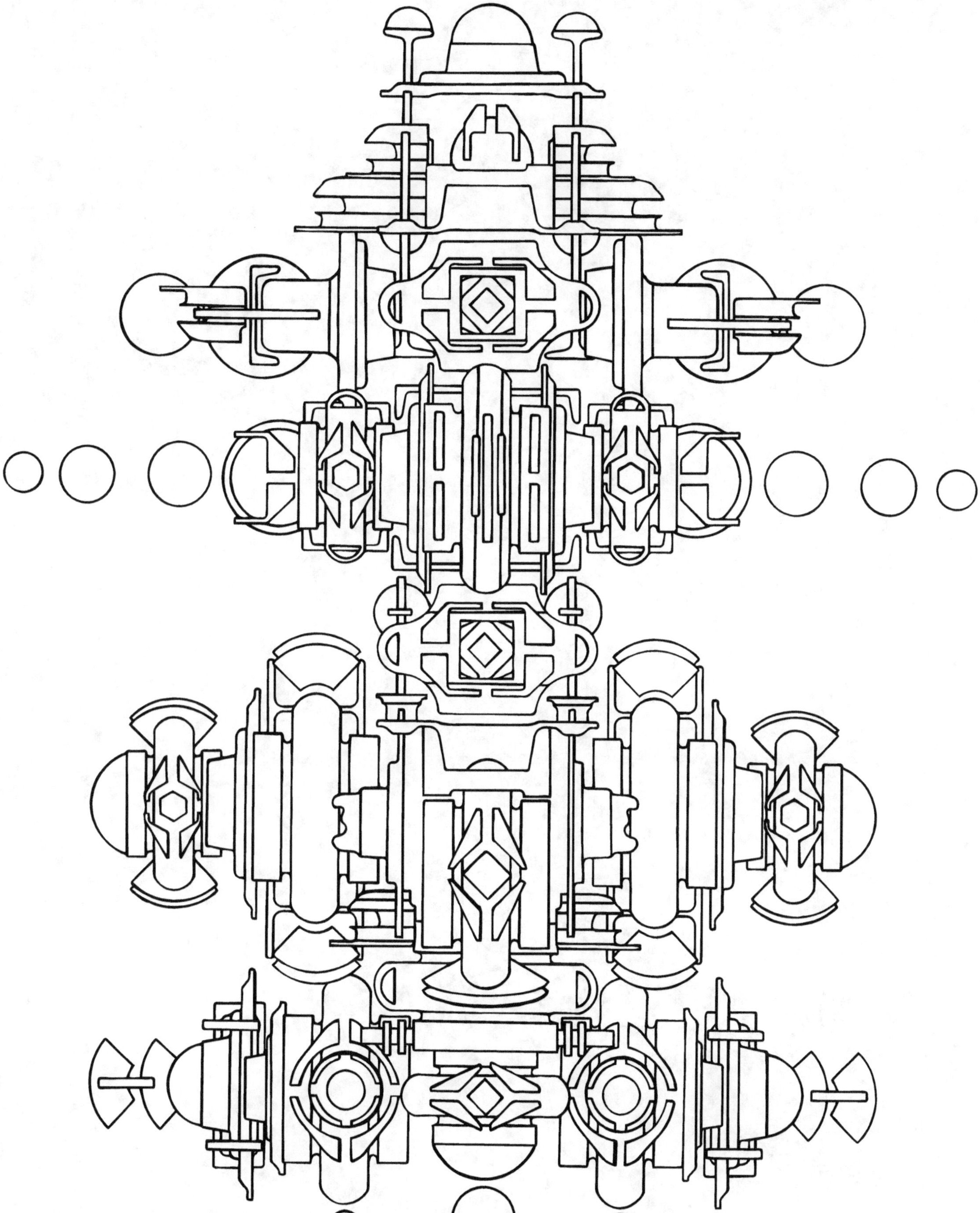

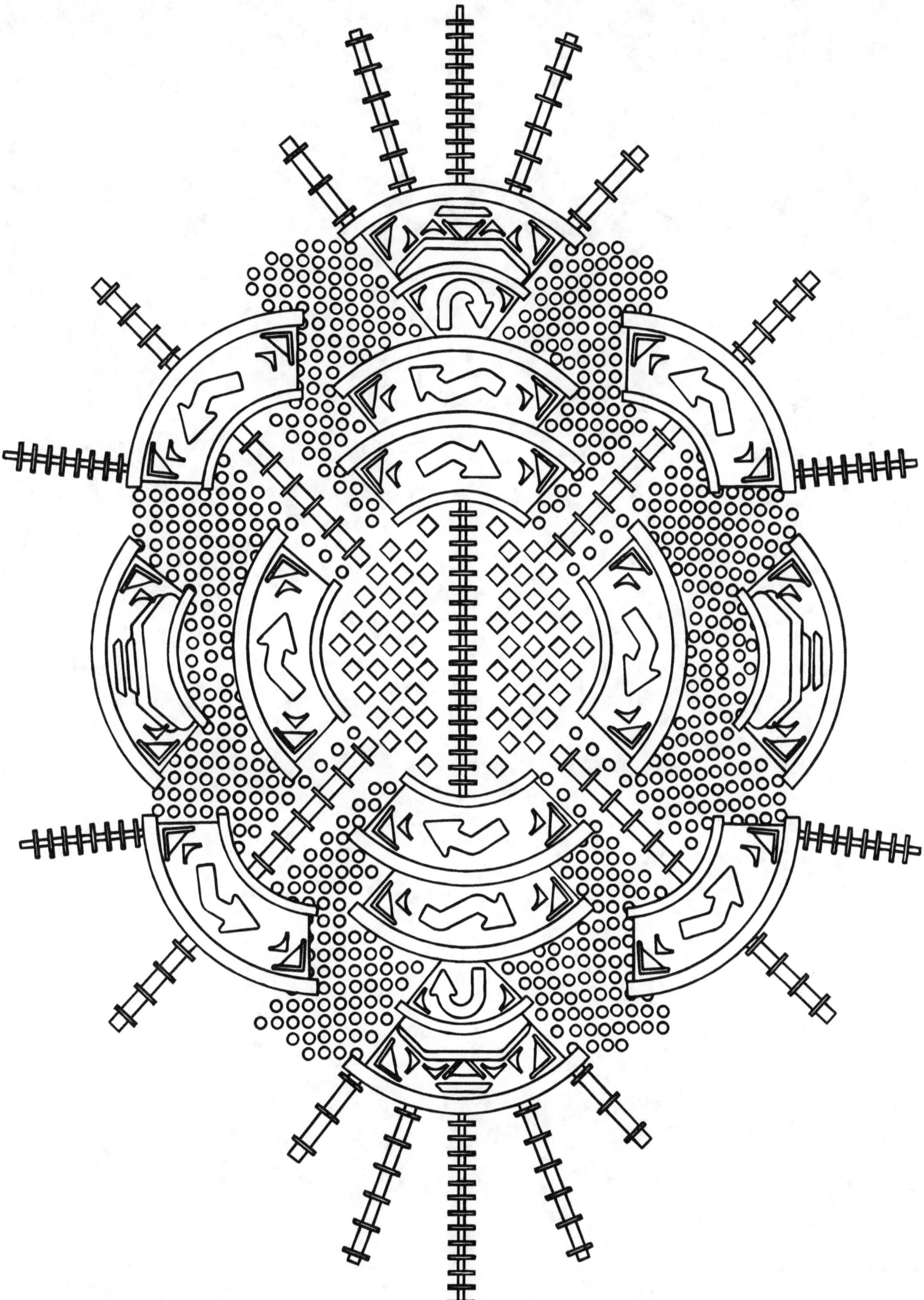

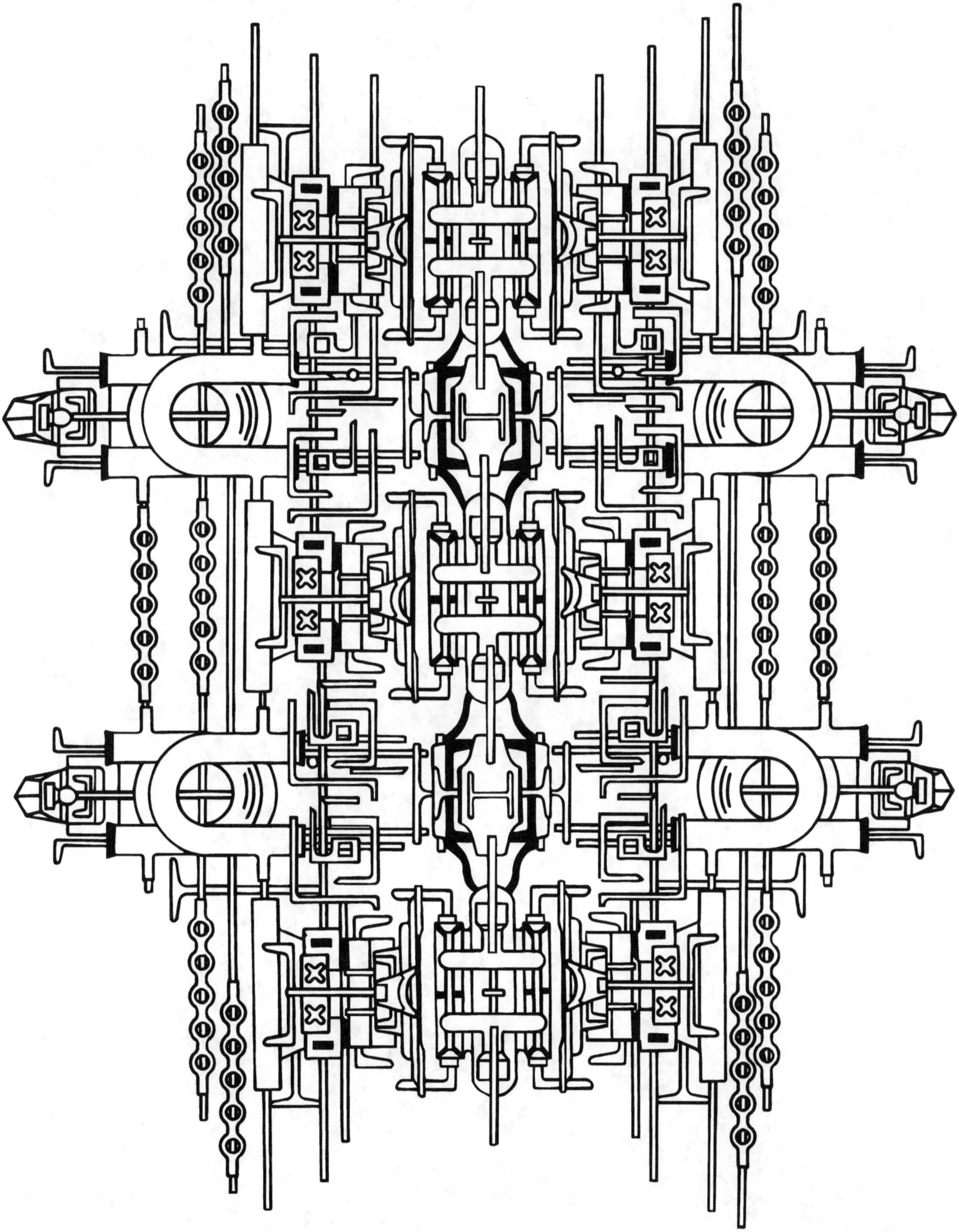

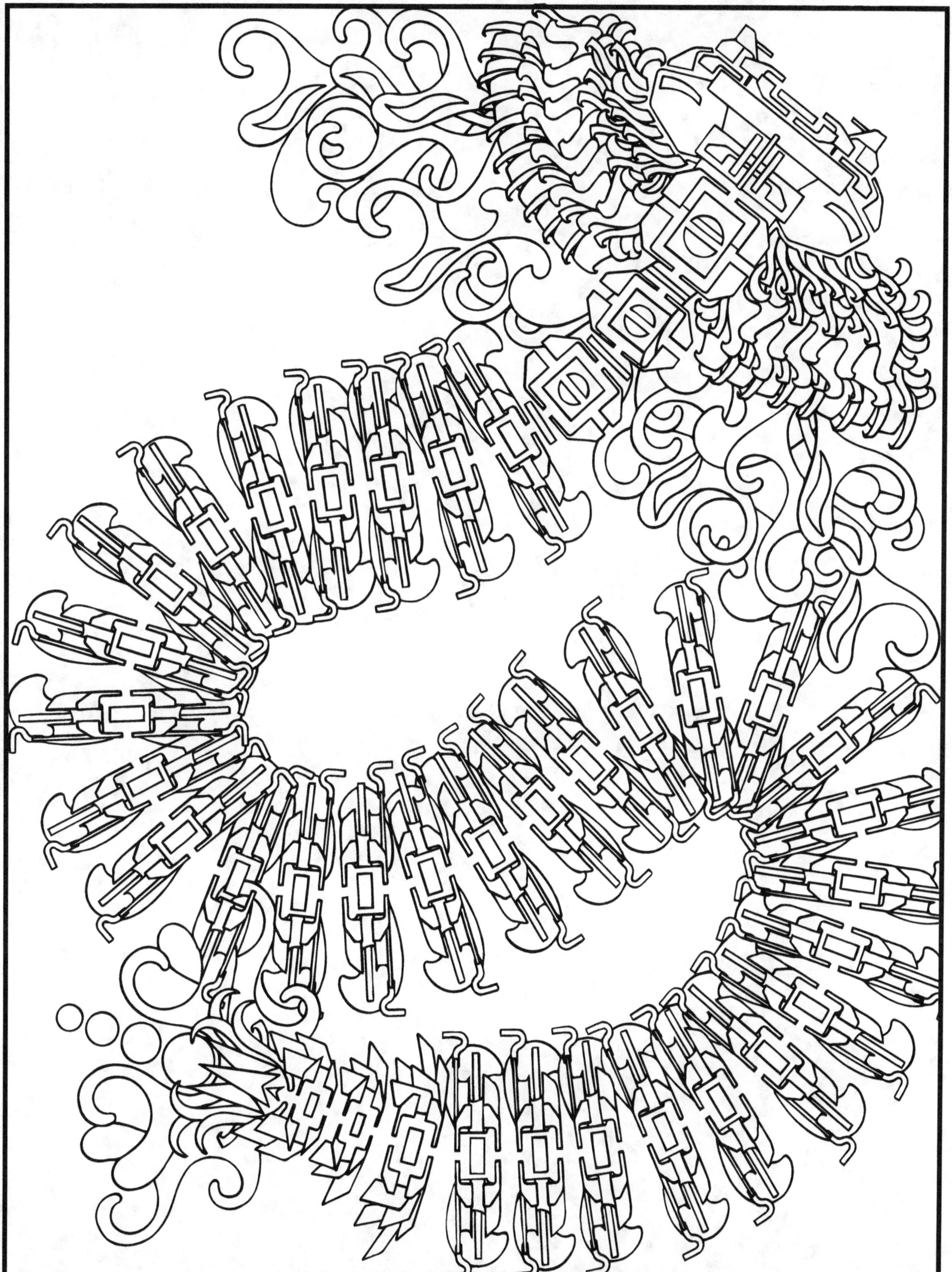

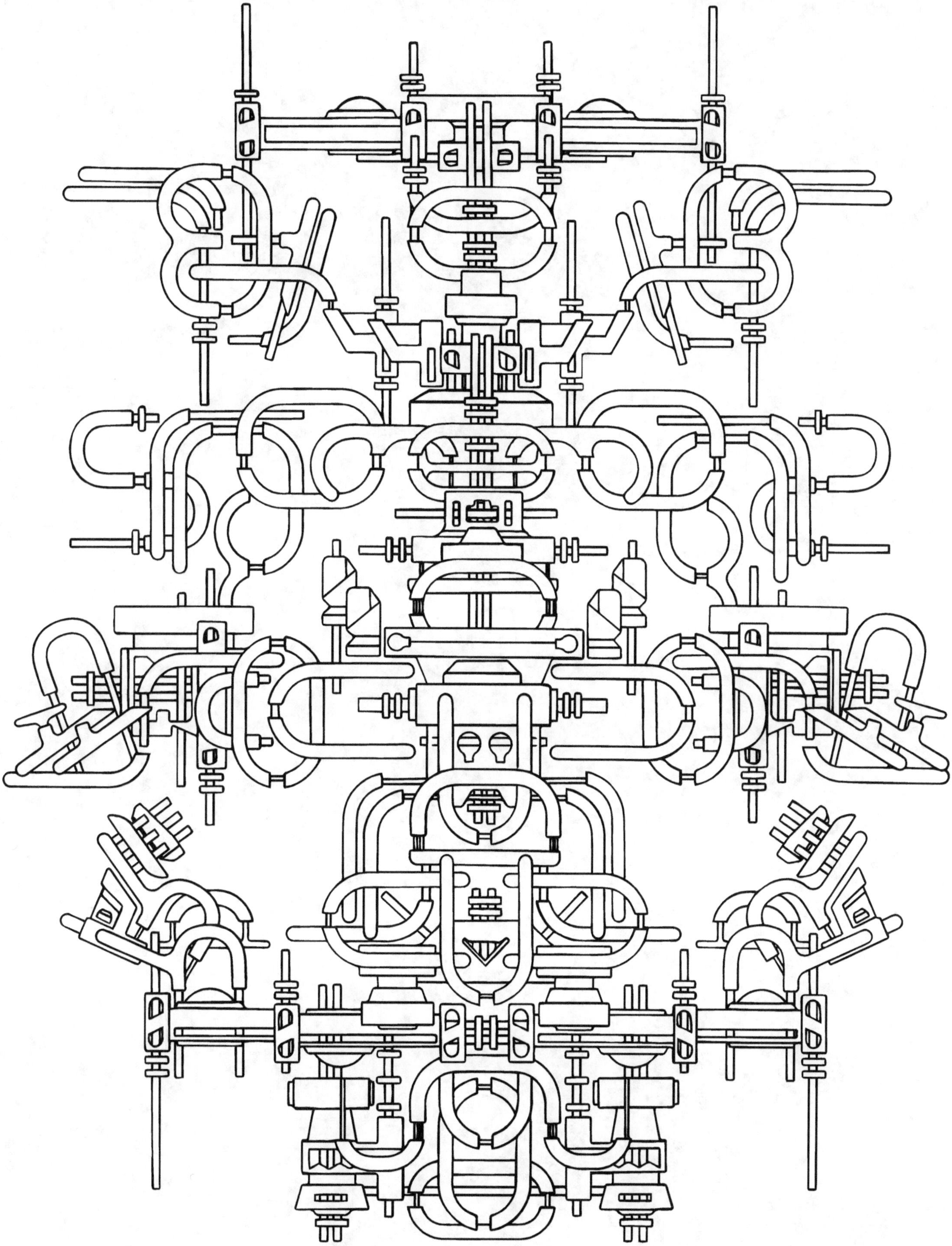

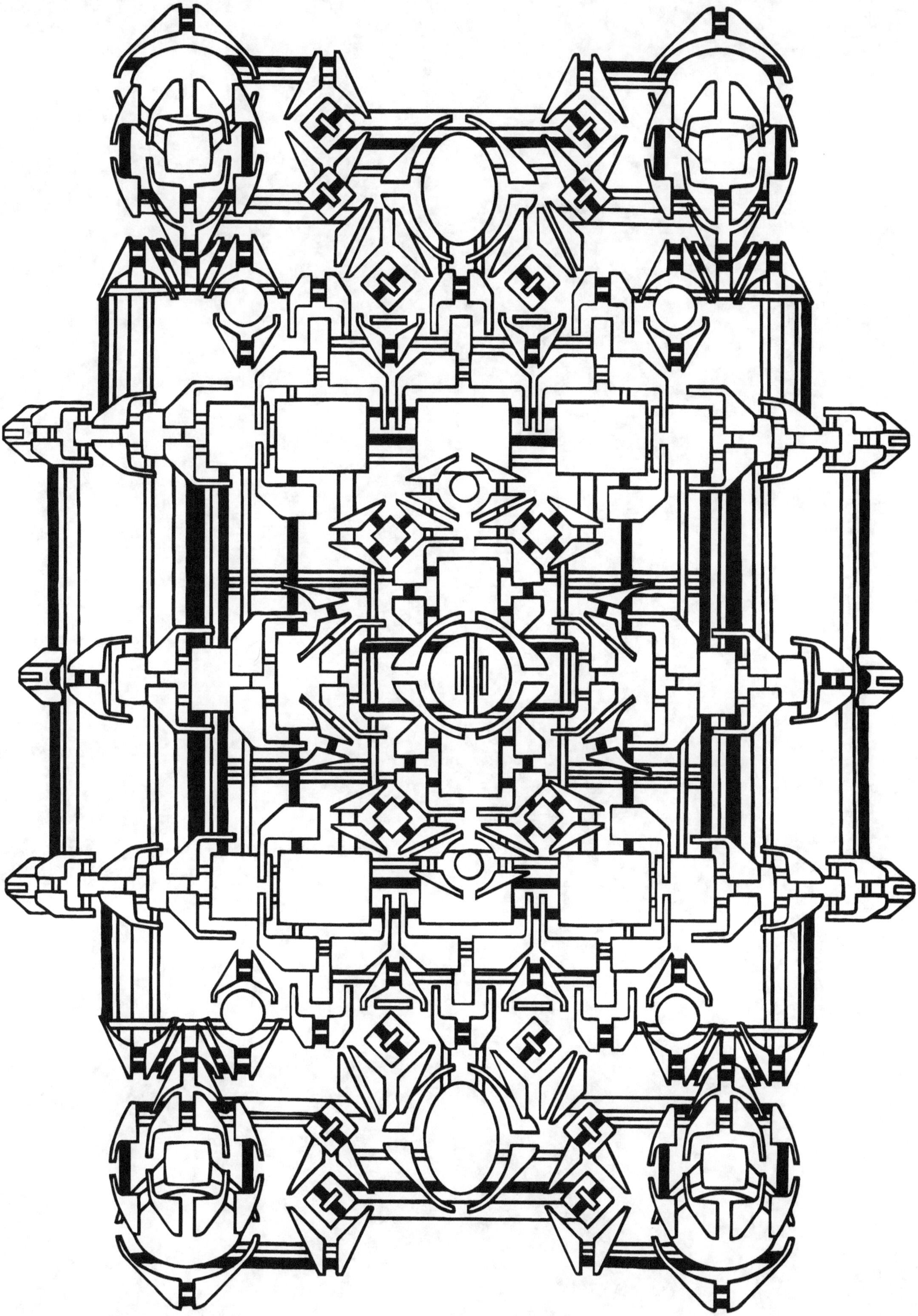

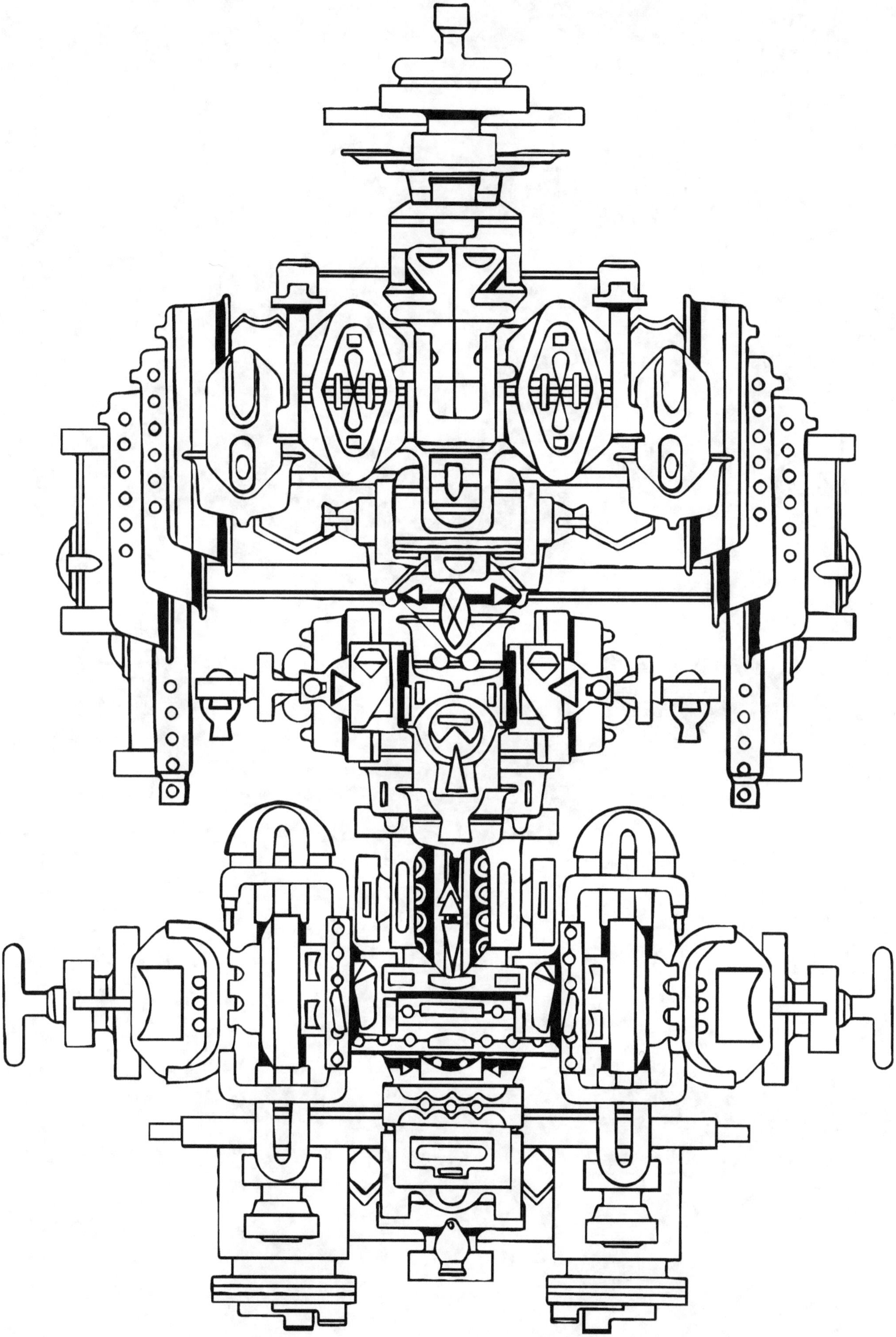

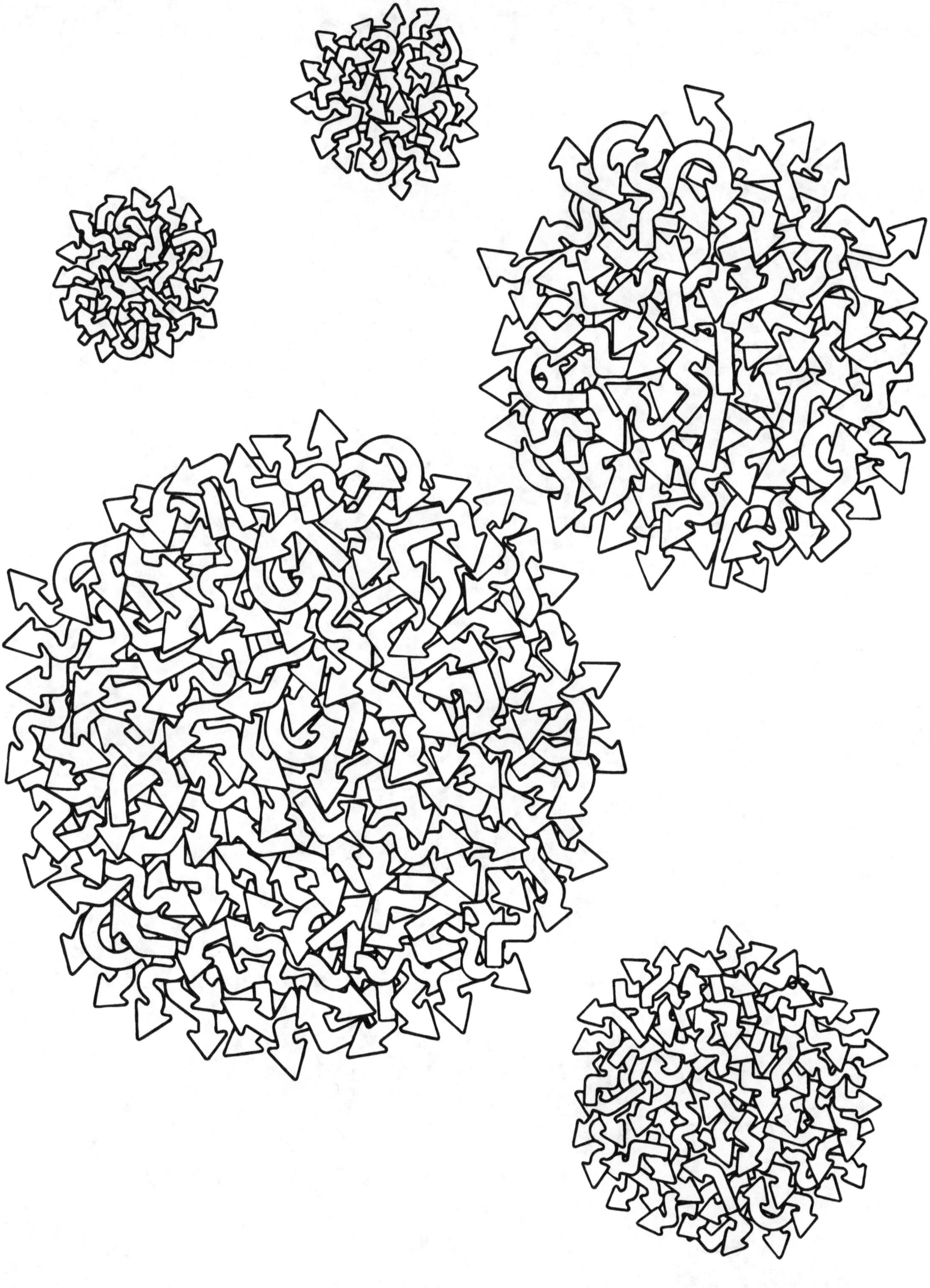

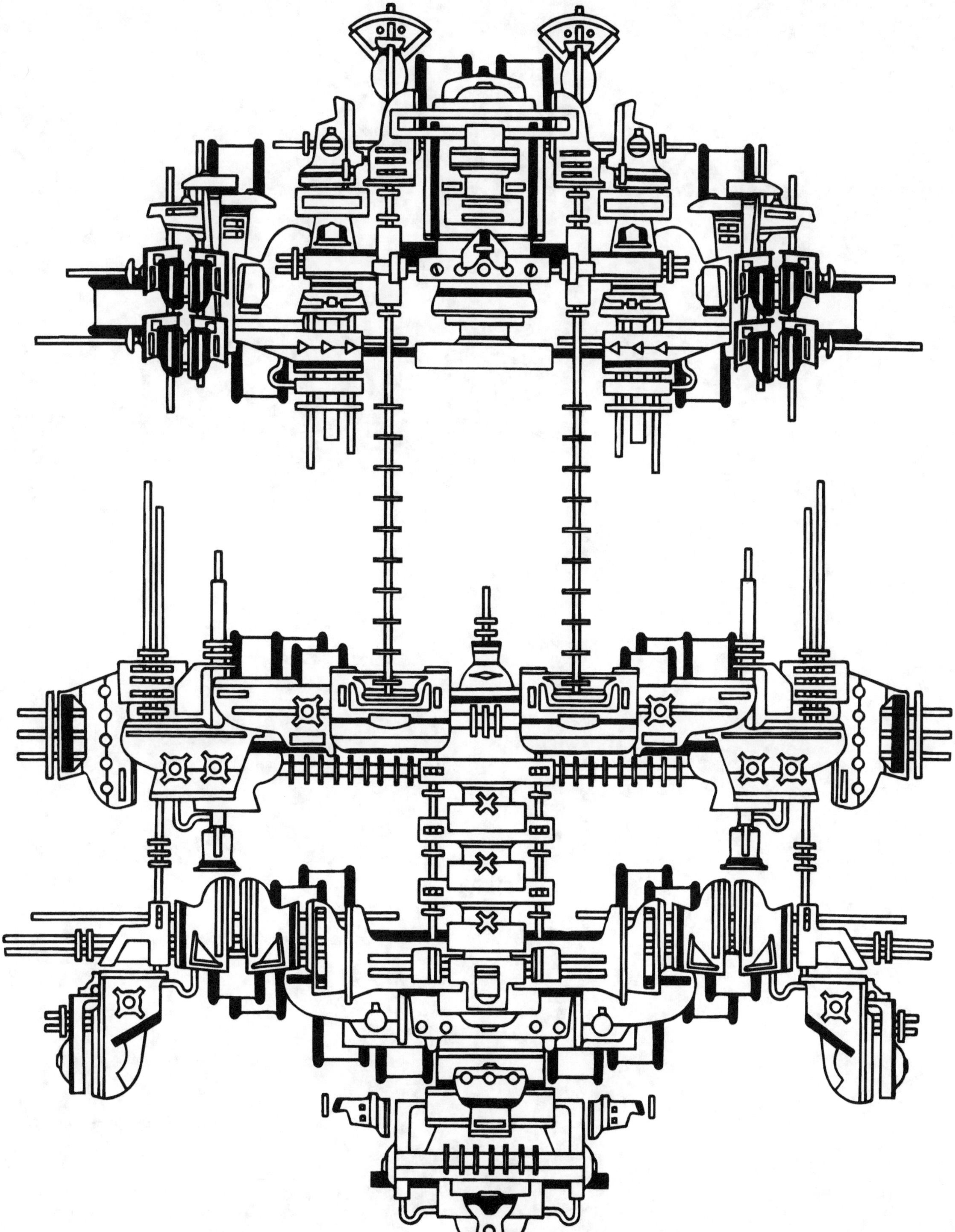

www.ingramcontent.com/pod-product-compliance
Lightning Source LLC
Chambersburg PA
CBHW081119180526
45170CB00008B/2928